TABLE OF CONTENTS

Contents

Contents

18 Plumbing 139

19 Pools and Hot Tubs 149

Contents

ABOUT THE AUTHOR

Lynda Lyday is a licensed contractor and a union carpenter in New York City. In the male-dominated field of carpentry, Lyday is considered a Renaissance woman for being one of the very few female carpenters to learn her trade through The United Brotherhood of Carpenters. Lyday worked side-by-side with the most talented woodworkers in the business, earning their trust and learning their trade secrets, making her one of the most respected finish carpenters in the business—regardless of her gender.

In 1985, Lyday—in her fourth year as an apprentice—won the Golden Hammer Award, which enabled her to become the first woman to teach carpentry at the New York City District Council of Carpenters Labor Technical College.

In the early 1990s, Lyday, by then a working licensed carpenter with her own construction company, started moonlighting at night, returning to her early theater roots by writing and performing in sketch comedy shows in New York City's vibrant cabaret scene.

The marriage of her skills as a carpenter and her ease in front of an audience caught the eye of The Discovery Channel's *Gimme Shelter* executives, who found her in 1997 and asked her to be one of their show's experts.

HGTV then hired Lyday to co-host *The Fix* for three seasons, which netted her an introduction to HGTV's sister station, The DIY Network, where, in 2001, she began cohosting *Talk2DIY Home Improvement* with Brad Staggs. Lyday also hosted *Best Built Home* on The DIY Network.

In total, since combining her skills as a carpenter and a performer, Lyday has hosted over 350 home improvement shows, as well as made numerous appearances on CNN, ABC, CBS, and NBC. She has also been featured on radio and in major print media.

Lyday's first book, *Lynda Lyday's Do It Yourself! The Room-by-Room, Step-by-Step Guide to the Most Popular Home Repair and Renovation Projects*, was published in April 2005 by Perigee Books. Lyday is also one of the featured professionals in the book *The Experts Guide to Life at Home*, scheduled for publication in October 2005.

Advancing the cause of female do-it-yourselfers worldwide, Lyday has created and designed her own tool line for women: Lyday Tool Line. The tools come with a smaller grip and are construction-grade quality formed to better fit a woman's hand, empowering women to tackle everyday household repairs on their own. Lyday Tool Line will be available online at www.Lyday.com, which will also direct you to local stores. To accompany her tool line, Lyday is currently designing her own clothing line, Lyday WorkWear, outfitting do-it-herselfers with comfortable clothing that fits the curves of a woman's body and supplying women with even more ammunition to demystify the home repair process.

DEDICATION

To all those who have worked hard to fulfill the dream of owning their own home.

ACKNOWLEDGMENTS

I have found writing a book is completely different from hanging a door! It wasn't until I started writing books that I realized how many people it takes to make me look good on paper!

I am grateful to have worked with the people at Que Publishing, who have made this process enjoyable. Everyone should be lucky enough to work with such a fine group of people. First, I want to thank the publisher, Paul Boger. Thanks to my acquisitions editor, Loretta Yates, who has been so reliable and attentive, making this journey a terrific experience. Thanks to Sean Dixon, my development editor, whose keen eye doesn't miss a thing and has terrific suggestions. Thanks to my project editor, Mandie Frank, who delicately cracked the whip, making sure the book hit its deadlines. Thanks to my technical editor, Ben Helmuth, for his logical thinking.

No one wants the job of the copy editor and proofreader when working on a book that I wrote, but Megan Wade has done a terrific job and must be very tired now! I also want to thank Aaron Black, who indexed the book. And thanks to Cindy Teeters, the publishing coordinator, for responding so quickly. Many thanks to the talented illustrator, Phil Velikan; designer Anne Jones; Kimberly Rogers in marketing; and Andrea Bledsoe, my publicist. Go Kim and Andrea!

A bundle of thanks to my family and friends who were understanding and supportive when I had to pass on parties and events because I needed to write. Many thanks to my mom and dad who are always my number one fans; Paul and Connie for watching the girls; Simon and Hangzhou Diversitech who have made my dream come true; Katherine for her endless support, love, and brains (and for that, I say "thank you!"); Don for his sense of humor and reminding me how far I've come; Heidi for her support and allowing me to talk tirelessly on her answering machine; Rose and Carol for their artistic eye and creative direction; fellow author Lisa for sharing her own experience; Cathleen for helping me step down from the ledge; and the many other friends who have been supportive.

We Want to Hear from You!

As the reader of this book, *you* are our most important critic and commentator. We value your opinion and want to know what we're doing right, what we could do better, what areas you'd like to see us publish in, and any other words of wisdom you're willing to pass our way.

As the publisher for Que Publishing, I welcome your comments. You can email or write me directly to let me know what you did or didn't like about this book—as well as what we can do to make our books better.

Please note that I cannot help you with technical problems related to the topic of this book. We do have a User Services group, however, where I will forward specific technical questions related to the book.

When you write, please be sure to include this book's title and author as well as your name, email address, and phone number. I will carefully review your comments and share them with the author and editors who worked on the book.

Email: feedback@quepublishing.com

Mail: Paul Boger
           Publisher
           Que Publishing
           800 East 96th Street
           Indianapolis, IN 46240 USA

For more information about this book or another Que Publishing title, visit our website at www.quepublishing.com. Type the ISBN (excluding hyphens) or the title of a book in the Search field to find the page you're looking for.

INTRODUCTION

The Homeowner's Manual fulfills a similar function to the manual for your car. This manual is not a "how-to" book to repair your home. Rather, it is a book designed to give you a roadmap of the materials used in your home along with terms associated with various materials, conditions, and systems. Like everything on this planet, the materials used to build your home have a lifespan, but with proper maintenance you can increase their longevity. *The Homeowner's Manual* helps you prevent and troubleshoot common house problems and determine when you need to call in the experts.

All homeowners are first-time buyers at one time in their lives, and most usually experience the insecurity of feeling inadequate about knowing how a home operates properly and the maintenance needed to keep it in good working order. You will learn quickly that the moment you own a home, you have plenty to do on your weekends and time off. This is the nature of owning a home. There is always something on the to-do list that needs to be fixed, a renovation that has been gnawing at you, or maybe even an add-on that needs to be completed. No matter what it is, I will help you understand the proper materials to use for your situation and whether you can tackle the project yourself or need to pick up the phone and call a pro.

Introduction

This book is designed to equip you with some overall knowledge on how the various systems work and integrate with each other. Some troubleshooting tips and repairs are addressed along with some design theories; however, I would suggest buying specialty books for home repair, design, landscaping, and so on if you plan on doing the work yourself. You will make some mistakes along the way, but let's face it, our mistakes are our best teachers. At least, they have been mine.

Congratulations on investing your money in a home. That is a wise investment, so be sure you protect its value. *The Homeowner's Manual* should help you with the big picture of owning a home, teach you about yearly and seasonal maintenance, and let you sound like a well-informed homeowner when talking to a professional.

The Big Picture
from A to Z

1

When you buy a home, you quickly learn that you have given yourself a weekend project for the length of that ownership because there is always something to clean, install, or repair. When my parents sold their home of 40 years, the house inspector said he had never seen a home in such good shape. That's because my parents fixed each problem immediately and kept their investment in good shape.

Proper maintenance of your home will keep your home working properly and cut down on bigger repairs in the future. First-time home buyers may not understand the scope of how a home functions and the various operating systems. *The Homeowner's Manual* is much like your car's manual. It is a handbook to give you an overall understanding of the operating systems and areas of your home and how they work together. It is important to know what you need to do to keep the various building materials in proper working order to lengthen their lifespans and what to do when damage occurs.

The Homeowner's Manual is divided into areas and systems to help you understand how a home operates and how the various areas work together. When everything is working properly, your home should feel comfortable and safe.

Chapter 1   The Big Picture from A to Z

Garage and Outbuildings

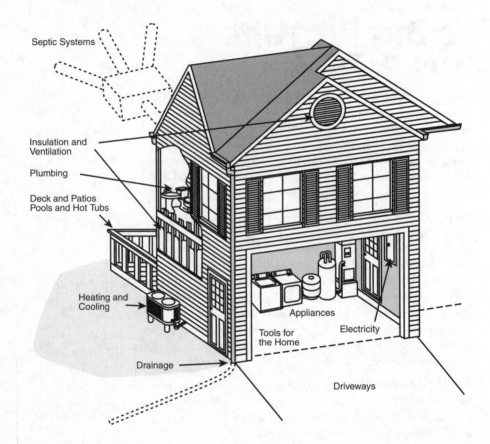

Septic Systems

Insulation and Ventilation

Plumbing

Deck and Patios Pools and Hot Tubs

Heating and Cooling

Appliances

Electricity

Tools for the Home

Drainage

Driveways

Appliances: Proper maintenance is the most important part of keeping your appliances in good working order.

Basements: The biggest problem basements have is moisture or water. There are various solutions to this problem.

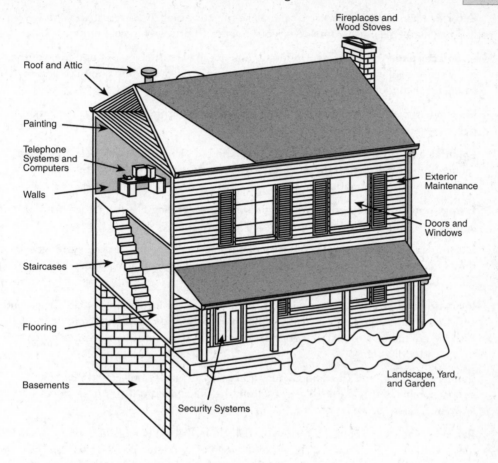

Fireplaces and Wood Stoves

Roof and Attic

Painting

Telephone Systems and Computers

Walls

Staircases

Flooring

Basements

Security Systems

Exterior Maintenance

Doors and Windows

Landscape, Yard, and Garden

Decks and Patios: There are different products and methods to keep your deck and patio in good condition and increase their life.

Doors and Windows: Weatherproof and seal doors and windows properly. Low-E glass and Energy Star windows and doors are more energy efficient and should be considered when remodeling. Know the proper location and size of an egress window.

Drainage: Keeping water away from your home is imperative. Proper grading and the installation of drains should be considered.

Driveways: Sealing, washing, and filling cracks in your driveway will increase its longevity.

Electricity: Get a general description of a home's electricity and the locations of circuit breakers or fuses. Understanding the basics of GFCI switches, codes, wattage, and light bulbs is important.

Exterior Maintenance: For curb appeal, keep your siding in tip-top shape. Know your building materials on the outside of your home and properly maintain them.

Fireplaces and Wood Stoves: Understanding the basics of chimneys and their proper maintenance will help you keep your fireplace or wood stove safe and efficient. Installing chimney caps is important to keep animals out.

Flooring: Knowing the proper cleaning, sealing, and finishing products is important to ensuring your floors' longevity.

Foundation: Know when to fill a crack and when to call an engineer. Learn to seal a foundation from water on the outside of your home, how to install foundation drains, and when to use foundation vents.

Garage and Outbuildings: Covers a general understanding of your garage door opener and how to keep it working properly. Also learn to remove oil from the floor.

Heating and Cooling: Learn the basics of a home's heating and cooling systems and their lifespans, including proper duct insulation, caulking, replacing filters, and cleaning coils.

Insulation and Ventilation: Know the proper R-Value for insulation in walls, attics, and crawlspaces, including batt insulation, blown insulation, and expandable foam insulation. Also covers the proper installation of baffles in the attic, soffit vents, gable vents, turbines, and roof vents.

Landscape, Yard, and Garden: Understand fertilizer, grass, mulch, and planting. Landscape for better water flow away from the house, and prevent fires by cutting low limbs and cleaning out brush.

Painting: Know your paints. Interior paints include flat, satin, eggshell, semi-gloss, hi-gloss, and primer. Learn the difference between oil and latex paint for use on the outside of your home. Also find out what prep work you need to do, including buying a mildew additive.

Plumbing: Get a general understanding of your home's plumbing: vents, drainage, and hot and cold supply. Learn how to handle a clog or an overflow; the locations of your valves; and about your hot water heater, including flushing it, replacing the anode rod, and controlling its temperature.

Pools and Hot Tubs: Maintaining your pool is important. Learn about vacuuming, filters, and getting the proper pH level. Also find out the lifespan of your pool lining.

Roof and Attic: Understand your roof and whether it has rafters or trusses. Learn about flat and pitched roofs and materials such as asphalt, clay, and slate tiles. Learn to clean off mildew, install zinc strips, check your gutters and downspouts, and install gutter guards. Find out what vent ridges, roof vents, and turbines are.

Security Systems: Covers the choices of security systems within your home.

Septic Systems: Understand the septic tank and its components, such as the holding tank, distribution tank, leech field, and gray water/biological waste. Learn how to find the location of your septic tank and how to perform routine maintenance, including pumping the tank and getting a professional inspection.

Staircases: Learn about handrails, newels, spindles, the stairs to your attic, and how to fix squeaky stairs.

Telephone Systems and Computers: Rotary, touch tone, and wireless phones differ, as do their lifespans. Learn about Internet connections such as the standard telephone line (dial-up), ISDN line (telephone line with three lines), ADSL (broadband), HST (satellite), cable ISP, and wireless Internet.

Tools for the Home: Get a list of tools for your home. Your starter kit should include a ladder, snow shovel, and similar items.

Walls: Detecting if your walls are made of plaster or drywall is important. Learn wall covering basics such as what to use for removal and repair, fixing nail pops, and using the proper insulation.

2

Appliances

There are many appliances we use in our homes. As with all things in life, there is a lifespan to each appliance. However, before you go out and buy a new one, try some troubleshooting first. Proper maintenance to your appliances will keep them in good working order, often years past their lifespan.

Hopefully, you have the manuals to your appliances. However, if you bought your home with the appliances already installed, the previous owner probably didn't give them to you. For those of you who do not have the owner's manuals, try going online and doing a search for the make and model of your appliance. Sometimes manufacturers provide manuals to download from the Web, while others will send you a copy.

Before you tackle any repair, always turn off the power to the appliance by unplugging it or cutting off the power at the breaker or fuse box. If you do not feel confident in doing any of the troubleshooting tips described in this chapter, hire a professional.

IN THIS CHAPTER

- Proper maintenance for your home's appliances, including the refrigerator, stove/range, oven, dishwasher, garbage disposal, trash compactor, washing machine, and dryer

- Troubleshooting and easy fixes

Refrigerator

Figure 2.1 shows the components of a refrigerator. A little maintenance from time to time will keep your refrigerator working properly and increase the longevity of this appliance:

- Clean the coils located in the rear or bottom of the refrigerator. Pull the unit straight out and vacuum the vents and coils to remove the dust that makes the appliance work harder to cool the inside of the refrigerator.

Chapter 2 Appliances

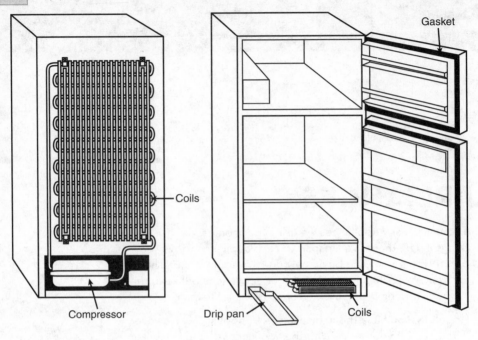

Coil placement (back)   Coil placement (underneath)

FIGURE 2.1

Components of a refrigerator.

- Clean the drip pan located beneath your refrigerator; it is easily removed from the front or from the back. In automatic defrost models, the water from the defrost process flows through a tube and lands in a pan or goes directly into a drain in the floor. The pan is located at the bottom of the refrigerator and can be removed from the rear or front, depending on the make and model. While you're at it, clean the tube because it can become plugged with food particles. Push a pipe cleaner into the tube to help remove all the particles. If the entire tube can be removed, flush it with soapy water and then clean it water.

- The gasket is the seal on the door that keeps the cold air from leaking out of the refrigerator. These tend to get a bit of dirt and grease buildup on them. Wipe the gasket down with soapy water and then rinse and dry it. Close the door on a piece of paper. If the paper falls down, you need to replace the entire gasket. Use petroleum jelly on the gasket to keep it from drying out.

- Keep the temperature of your refrigerator between 36°F and 38°F. The freezer should stay between 0°F and 5°F. If you do not have an automatic defroster, you must defrost your freezer regularly to keep the freezer coils working properly. Do not let ice build up more than 1/4" thick. When it reaches this level, defrost your freezer. Remove all the frozen items and defrost the freezer quickly according to the manufacturer's directions. I've always put pots of hot water in the freezer to help it defrost. Never use a sharp object to remove the ice. One wrong move and you will puncture the coils, letting all the gas escape—and your freezer will no longer keep your food frozen.

- If the icemaker has stopped working, check to see if the little wire in the icemaker bin inside the freezer is up or down. If the wire is up, it automatically stops making ice. Move the wire down to engage the icemaker.

- If your icemaker is producing ice poorly, you may have a clog in the line attached to the back of the refrigerator. Turn off the water supply valve and check to see if there is anything obstructing the line or if it has been pinched. Replace the tubing if necessary.

- The lifespan of a refrigerator is about 17 years.

STOVE/RANGE

Daily cleaning of your stove or range will keep it looking nice and working properly; plus, there's nothing worse than a buildup of hardened cooking grease and ick to clean! Here are a few cleaning and maintenance tips:

- Most boiler pans are porcelain-coated steel and need to be cleaned with a nonabrasive cleanser. You can always buy replacement pans when your pan is beyond help.

- Most modern stove/oven control panels are made of glass or painted metal. Use a nonabrasive cleanser on these surfaces. Never spray a cleanser directly onto the control panel; instead, apply some on a damp cloth and wipe the surface.

- A porcelain cook top can be cleaned with a nonabrasive cleanser. A ceramic or glass cook top needs to be cleaned with a special cleanser made for these cook tops.

- Soak the burner drip pans, which are beneath the grates in a gas stove, in soapy water to remove grease buildup. After a few years it is impossible to remove all the stains, so I suggest buying new drip pans. Bring the make and model of your appliance to a parts center to order new ones.

- Clean your knobs by removing them and soaking them in warm, soapy water. If your knobs do not come off, wipe them thoroughly with soapy water and a rag. You can buy replacement knobs if the writing has worn off them.

- For electric stoves, replace the burner coil if it stops working. Always turn off the power or unplug the stove at the outlet before removing the burner coil.

- Gas stoves may experience a gas flow problem. Check the holes around the burner because they can get clogged with grease and food. Use a toothpick to unclog these holes.

- Adjust the pilot light to the stove using a screwdriver on the adjustment screw. Keep the pilot light at about 3/8".

- If you smell gas or think your stove is not working properly, call a professional. If you smell gas, open the windows and call the gas company immediately.

- The lifespan of a stove or range is 14–19 years.

Ovens

Most ovens require a cleaning from time to time and a change of a light bulb after a few years. Generally, you will need to call a professional if your oven isn't working properly, but here are some maintenance tips to check before you pick up that phone:

- Light bulbs wear out in the oven just like they do in lamps. Check the manual to your appliance for proper removal and replacement. Most times, you will need to remove a glass covering before you can reach the bulb. Bulbs are usually 40-watt appliance bulbs.

- If you have a self-cleaning oven, check the manufacturer's manual on how to use this feature. It usually heats an oven so hot that it burns off any residue inside the oven.

- For ovens that aren't self-cleaning, use an oven cleaner and follow the manufacturer's directions.

- Electric ovens have a bake/boiler element that can easily be replaced. Check the manufacturer's manual for proper removal and replacement, and always work safely by unplugging the appliance or turning it off at the breaker box.

- Gas ovens have one or two burner tubes—newer models have two. Check to see if the holes in the burner tubes are free of grease and soot. Shut off the gas at the valve before poking a toothpick into the holes to clean them.

- From time to time, the pilot light can go off in a gas oven. If your oven isn't heating, check the pilot light. Turn off the gas, open a window, and make sure no gas is left in the oven before you light the pilot light.

- The lifespan of an oven is 14–19 years.

DISHWASHER

Figure 2.2 shows the components of a dishwasher. Here are several troubleshooting and maintenance tips to keep your dishwasher working properly:

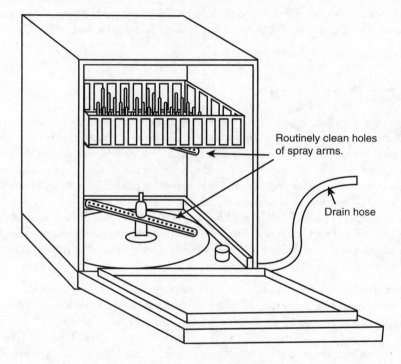

Routinely clean holes of spray arms.

Drain hose

FIGURE 2.2

Components of a dishwasher.

- Clean the filter regularly. The filter is located under the lower spray arm. Replace it if it has holes in it to protect the pump and motor from debris that may be in your dishwasher. Check your dishwasher's manual for proper removal.

- Clean the small holes in the spray arm if they become clogged with paper, food, and so on. The dishwasher will clean your dishes better if the water can easily come out all the holes of the sprayer arm.

- When the dishwasher doesn't drain properly, it is because of a clog in the drain line. Usually the clog is at the joint where the drain line attaches to the household drain line or garbage disposal. Remove the line and clear the debris from the hose. Reattach it and try it again.

- Some models have a belt that spins the motor. These belts can break down and need to be replaced.

- If the motor doesn't work, make sure you have power to the unit. If you do, but the dishwasher still doesn't work, then it is time to buy a new one.

- The lifespan of a dishwasher is about 10 years.

Garbage Disposer

The garbage disposer is one of my favorite appliances. (The more common term for this is *garbage disposal*, but that's a brand name. *Garbage disposer* is the more "proper" term, so that's the one I'll use here.) These usually work properly for a long time, provided you know what to put down them. Most vegetables can be cut and disposed of, but stringy items such as celery and meat should not be put in a disposer. There was a myth years ago that putting glass down a disposer and chopping it up would clean the blades. Can you imagine? NEVER PUT GLASS DOWN YOUR DISPOSER. If you want to clean the grease off your garbage disposer's blades, put some ice it in and run the disposer. Remember to always run the water while running the motor. The following are some other garbage disposer maintenance tips:

- If the unit hums when you turn on the switch, there's a good chance that an object is jamming it. Immediately turn off the switch. Be sure you have turned off the breaker before you work on any appliance. Use the Allen wrench (usually 1/4") that comes with the machine, and insert it into the port at the bottom of the unit. (These are called the *jam key* and the *jam key port*, as shown in Figure 2.3.) Turn the wrench back and forth to dislodge whatever has jammed the disposer. Stick your hand inside to see if you can lift out the object causing the jam (be careful not to cut yourself on the blades), or you can use a flashlight and a grabbing tool to remove the object. (Spring grabber tools are available at most hardware stores.)

- You may need to replace the rubber gasket between the disposer and the sink if you experience a leak.

- Hit the reset button, which is a little red switch located on the bottom of the unit (see Figure 2.3), if the unit doesn't turn on when you flip the switch.

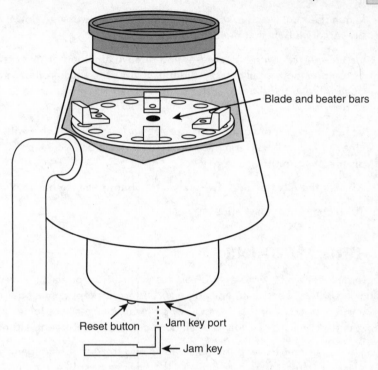

Blade and beater bars

Reset button   Jam key port

Jam key

FIGURE 2.3

The garbage disposer's jam key port and reset button locations.

- If the unit is grinding poorly, it may be time to replace it.

- If you experience a clog, you might want to remove and check the dishwasher's hose at the bottom of the disposer for an obstruction.

- The lifespan of a garbage disposer is about 10 years.

TRASH COMPACTOR

My trash compactor has always been my foot, but if you have this convenient appliance, here are some maintenance tips:

- If your trash compactor stops working, check to see if it is plugged in. Make sure the outlet is working by plugging in a radio or other item you know works. Reset the ground fault switch if you have a GFCI outlet. There could be a problem with the switch and possibly something obstructing the door so it doesn't close properly.

- When the ram, which is what compacts the trash, won't go down, there may be a broken drive belt that needs to be replaced.

- Clean the track with a degreaser and remove any food or objects to allow the drawer to open more easily. Spray a lubricant over the track, rollers, and glides. If that doesn't make the drawer easier to open, then you might need to replace the rollers or tracks.

- Clean the inside of your compactor regularly and thoroughly with an antibacterial cleaner. This will help remove odors. After it has been cleaned, spray a germ-killing disinfectant on the inside of it.

- Change the filter once or twice a year if your appliance has one.

- Trash compactors last about 10 years.

Washing Machine

I can never seem to write about troubleshooting tips for washing machines without thinking of the *I Love Lucy* episode where the suds kept coming out of the machine. I mistakenly re-created that episode when I was younger and doing laundry on my own. So, the first tip is to use the right amount of laundry detergent! Here are some others:

- Level your unit to keep the noise down and to keep it from damaging parts in the machine. Keep the unit as close to the floor as possible when leveling it.

- If your machine has a lint filter, you will need to clean it periodically. Check your owner's manual if you do not see the lint filter on the top of the tub.

- The water hoses that come with your unit will eventually wear out and need to be replaced when they leak or burst.

- If the machine does not turn on, check to see if it is plugged in and that the circuit breaker is on or the fuse is good.

- If the washer spins but doesn't remove the water, an item such as a sock might be stuck in the drain line. Remove the drain line from the pump and remove the item. Reattach the line to the pump and try again. If this doesn't fix it, call a professional. Your pump may need to be replaced.

- If the washer won't spin, it might need a new lid switch or pump—or it might need a new pump belt if you hear the motor running. I suggest calling a professional if you have any of these problems.

- If the machine won't spin or agitate, you might need a new lid switch.

DRYER

As much as I love my dryer, I have to say that I love the way clothes smell after they've dried on a clothesline. Plus, there's no maintenance required for a clothesline. A dryer, on the other hand, requires some maintenance for it to work properly. With this appliance, you don't want to cut corners on regular maintenance and cleaning because, if the air doesn't flow out of it properly, it can start a fire because of the heat. Here are some troubleshooting and maintenance procedures:

- If the dryer won't turn on, you need to check that it is plugged in and that the circuit breaker is on. Make sure you check to see if the outlet is working. If the door switch is defective, the dryer will not turn on. Replace the door switch with the power off.

- Many dryers have a heat-sensitive thermal fuse that is mounted at the exhaust duct inside the cover panel at the back. The fuse is embedded with a black resin and mounted in a white plastic housing. Replace the fuse, but before you use your dryer, inspect the venting system to make sure there is nothing obstructing the flow of hot air out.

- The vent pipe should be made of aluminum and needs to be cleaned if you notice that your clothes are not drying properly or the unit is overheating. Unplug the unit, remove the vent pipe at the back of the dryer, and check to see if there is any buildup. Clean it if necessary. You should do this at the elbow joints and the outside portion of the vent. You might need to remove a vent cap or screen to be able to feel inside the vent. Lint buildup can cause the heat to build up, possibly causing a fire. Always vent your dryer outside in as short a distance as possible. You do not want a bunch of turns in the vent pipe because too many bends cause a fire hazard. Always follow the manufacturer's installation instructions for the vent.

- Clean the lint filter after every drying cycle, and replace the filter if you notice any rips or tears. Dryer sheets and fabric softeners can clog the lint filter. From time to time, wash the filter in the sink or bathtub with soapy water and a soft-bristle brush.

- Clean or vacuum the chute the lint filter sits in. If you have a severe case of lint buildup, hire a professional to take the unit apart to clean it.

- Once the heating element has quit working in your electric dryer, you will need to replace it.

- The lifespan of a dryer is about 10 years.

HOT WATER HEATER

See Chapter 18, "Plumbing," for information on hot water heaters.

CHECKLIST

❑ First check to see if your appliance is plugged in if it is not working.

❑ Before investigating or fixing your appliances, turn off the power by unplugging it or turning off the breaker.

❑ Clean the refrigerator coils and drip pan and the fill tube in ice makers.

❑ Clean your stove or oven with the products suggested by the manufacturer.

❑ Call the gas company if you smell gas leaking from your stove or oven. Shut off the gas valve that feeds the appliance immediately and open the windows or doors.

❑ Clean the drain hose on a dishwasher if it's clogged. Check the holes on the sprayer arm to make sure they are open.

❑ Use a jam key (Allen wrench) if your garbage disposer is clogged. Push the reset button if it isn't working at all. Never put your hand in the disposer without its power cut off at the breaker or fuse box.

❑ Keep your trash compactor clean and free of debris in the tracks.

❑ Check the washing machine's drain hose if it is clogged and not draining properly.

❑ Check the dryer's lint tray and clean it after each drying cycle.

❑ Keep the dryer vents clear of lint.

❑ Always call a professional if the job is above your ability.

3

BASEMENTS

I grew up in Atlanta, where everyone had basements. Personally, I love a house with a basement. My cousins, on the other hand, grew up in Florida where basements are rare in the home. I always felt bad for my cousins until one night we got such a bad rainstorm that we were up all night removing the 5" of water that had puddled up in our basement. This was before wet vacuums existed, so our family became an assembly line of buckets and wet rags. It was then when I realized why my mom said to my aunt that she should be happy she didn't have a basement.

Homes that were built in the 1970s and earlier have minimal waterproofing or sealing. As techniques have gotten better and building codes gotten stricter, we've ended up with better-built homes that today are energy efficient and deal with the home as an integrated system of proper airflow, insulation, and moisture control. But, for many of us who've bought a fixer-upper or an older home, leaks or moisture is a problem. My experience has been that the longer this issue isn't addressed, the worse the problem will get down the line.

WATER

The most common enemy of a basement is water. Whether your basement suffers from water seeping in through the walls and floors or condensation buildup, it can wreak havoc for a home. Many people associate a basement with a dank, musty odor, and where there is a musty odor there is mold. Mold has become such a problem that there are multimillion dollar businesses popping up to properly tackle and remove mold from a home. I remember a case where a million-dollar home had to be bulldozed because of mold.

Water and condensation can also cause wood to rot. Often, the wood jambs and thresholds are the first to go. Moisture also makes a great environment for termites to have a smorgasbord. So, removing water and moisture from your basement is serious business.

There are a few ways to deal with the moisture or water that gets into your basement. You may want to hire a home inspector to give you his opinion on the matter and the best way to tackle the situation. Waterproofing companies deal with this issue, too. However, some of these companies will push one method when you might need more than that. First, figure out if it is a leak or a moisture problem.

Leaking or Condensation

Water leaking in or condensation? A quick test to determine if you are having a water leak through your wall is to tape a piece of plastic or tin foil to the wall where you suspect water is coming in (see Figure 3.1). Make sure you tape down all the sides, and then wait a few days. If beads of moisture have formed on the inside of the foil/plastic and between it and the wall, you have a leak coming through that wall. If there is moisture on the outside of the foil/plastic, your basement is suffering from a moisture problem.

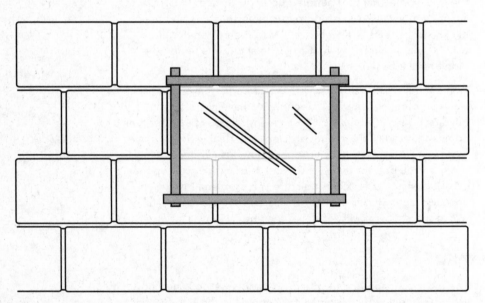

FIGURE 3.1

Tape a piece of plastic to a wall to check for leaks and moisture.

Condensation is a result of too much moisture in the air. When warm air touches a glass of iced tea in the summer, the cool glass brings down the temperature of the air around it, drawing out the moisture which sits on the outside of the glass. Similarly, when there is too much moisture in your home or basement, the coolness of the walls pulls the moisture out of the air and the water droplets sit on the walls, metal, and other cool surfaces, creating a damp basement.

Condensation Solutions

Many people are not aware that a family's living habits create moisture in the air. This moisture needs to be dealt with by using proper ventilation. (See Chapter 15, "Insulation and Ventilation," for more information on ventilating your home.) The following can put moisture into the air: a clothing line, a dryer, cooking, showers, and dew in the air. The following tips will help you keep condensation from becoming a problem:

- First, if you are drying clothes on a line in your basement, move them to the outdoors in the warmer months.

- If your washer and dryer are in your basement, make sure your dryer is vented properly and the vent is clear of any obstructions or lint build-up. Make sure there are no holes in the vent allowing moist air to leak into your living space. Check for leaks by feeling around the vent when the dryer is on. Every three years, take the vent apart and clean the lint build-up. The vent should be made of a 4" metal pipe and should exit your house close to the dryer. If you notice your clothes are not drying, you might have a clogged vent and should clean it as soon as possible.

- Clean your lint tray often and wash it with soapy water and a stiff brush to remove any dryer sheet buildup.

- Check your plumbing pipes and make sure there are no leaks coming from sinks or toilets up above.

- If you have a shower in the basement, make sure you install a fan and vent it properly.

- Check your air conditioner's drain pan and drain line for leaks or clogs. The drain line can become clogged due to algae or debris that will back into the drain pan. It won't take much for the drain pan to fill up and start to spill over. If this happens, you may want to call a professional to service the unit. For central air conditioning units, this drain line will look like it comes out of the furnace.

TIP

To check for leaky plumbing, go underneath your sinks and feel around the pipes for moisture. Check directly around the basin and then around the tailpipe and the P-trap. The P-trap is the bend in the pipe that looks like a *P*. Drain gasses cannot pass the P-trap because it allows for water to settle at the bottom, forming a seal. The P-trap also traps objects such as rings so they don't get washed away...usually! Be sure to regularly check for leaks; it only takes a few moments, and it's better to be safe than sorry. Often, we have no clue there is a loose fitting below the sink until the cabinet has rotted or, worse, it leaks into the basement below.

If condensation is not that big of a problem, you may have an air circulation problem. Sometimes homes are buttoned up so tightly that there isn't proper airflow. If you have central air conditioning, you can install more vents leading into your basement. This is relatively easy and should help a minor moisture problem. You can also use an exhaust fan to help remove moisture and create airflow. Remember, for the basement to have proper airflow, the air must have room to move. If you have a lot of clutter, maybe now is the time to have a yard sale or remove the clutter.

Personally, I would install a dehumidifier. This is a very proactive way to remove moisture. To determine if your basement needs a dehumidifier, see whether you have any of the following conditions:

- Condensation on the windows

- Mold

- Musty smells and stuffiness

- Rotting wood

- Wet stains on ceilings or walls

TIP

Next time it rains, put on your slicker and go outside. Check the gutters to see if they are properly catching rainwater. Then check the downspout to make sure it is diverting the water safely away from the home. Is there water puddling near the house? Does an area need to be built up with soil to alleviate puddling? Is the landscape sloped toward your home, bringing water up against the walls? Is water getting in through a stairwell or window well?

Leaky Basements

The second way a basement gets moisture is through ground water. Most people have water coming in from the walls or floors of their basements. When rainwater runs into your house, this is called *hydro-static*, or water pressure. The water can crack a foundation, leading to many ways in which water can penetrate through the walls. This is a bigger problem and one that first needs to be addressed from the outside of the house. How and why is water getting in?

Once you get to know what is going on during a hard rain, you can start to address the problem. Let's start from the top.

GUTTERS AND DOWNSPOUTS

Gutters are extremely important to catch water and then divert it away from your home (see Figure 3.2). Always make sure your gutters and downspouts are clear of any obstructions. Leaves, sticks, nuts, dirt, and granules from asphalt shingles can cause obstructions. Last year I cleaned my parent's gutters, which were filled with debris. Out of three downspouts, one of them was completely filled with debris, turning the gutter into a small waterfall onto the side of the house. Check to see that the gutters are installed properly. They must be tight against the fascia of your roof. If the gutter is pulled away, water can go directly down the wall. Make sure the shingles have been installed with enough overhang to spill the water down into the gutters. You can always install a piece of metal or flashing called a *drip edge* that goes under the shingle and curls over and into the gutter to make sure the water goes directly into the gutter.

Next, check out the downspouts. Make sure that these downspouts are directed a few feet away from the house and keeping the water away from the foundation.

You may want to have a landscaper help you with connecting downspouts to an underground drainage system.

→ For more information about your gutters, **see** "Drainage," **p. 166**.

> **CAUTION**
>
> Use a sturdy ladder and always have a helper hold the ladder in place. If you are not comfortable on a ladder or your home is too high, make sure you hire someone to do this. Never go up on a steep roof without a safety harness and proper length rope secured to a chimney or something that will hold your weight.

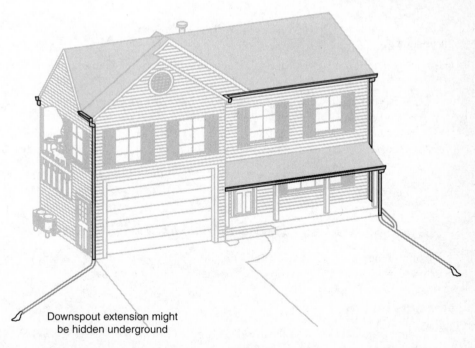

Downspout extension might
be hidden underground

FIGURE 3.2

The gutter drain system removing water from the house.

23

LANDSCAPING/GRADING

Sometimes the easiest fix is to properly slope your yard so that the water isn't puddling against your house (see Figure 3.3). Where you have puddling in your yard, you will need to fill it up with soil to help channel the water away from the house.

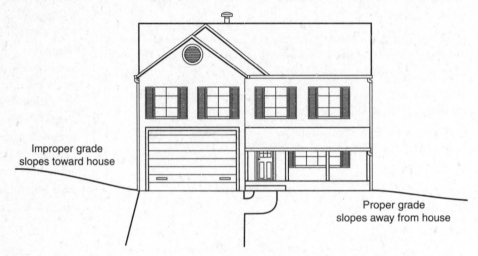

Improper grade slopes toward house

Proper grade slopes away from house

FIGURE 3.3

Improper grading that slopes toward a home needs to be removed and filled.

Check your patios, driveways, and paths. Again, they need to slope away from the house. You may need to check with a landscaper or a contractor to take a look at a patio or driveway that is not sloped properly. Depending on the integrity of your patio or driveway, you can apply a new layer of mortar, brick, or flagstone on the old slab.

Look where your driveway or patio meets your home. The sealant can crack over time due to extreme weather conditions or age. Remove the old sealant and replace it with new.

FRENCH DRAINS AND FOUNDATION DRAINS

Sometimes we have to live with a neighbor's landscape. If you are below a neighbor's yard, then you will be getting double the amount of rainwater.

French Drains

One of the best ways to divert water is by a French drain (see Figure 3.4). A French drain traditionally is a trench with gravel in it to catch water and channel it away from your home.

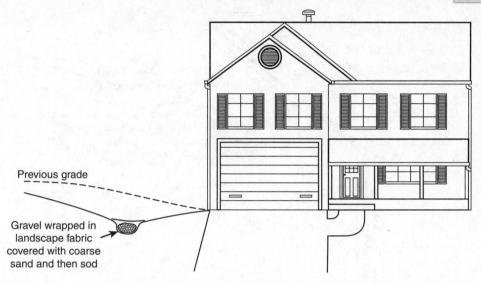

Previous grade

Gravel wrapped in
landscape fabric
covered with coarse
sand and then sod

FIGURE 3.4

A French drain catches water and channels it away from your home.

Find a place on your property at the bottom of the slope where you can horizontally catch the water and safely divert it away from your home. You don't want to spill water into another neighbor's home.

You should dig a French drain 8"–12" deep and 6" wide. You fill the trench with landscape fabric, pour in gravel, and wrap the gravel with the fabric creating a tube to keep out the dirt. Then shovel in some coarse sand and finish it off with sod.

Foundation Drains

Foundation drains are installed at the bottom of the foundation to divert the water that gathers around the house (see Figure 3.5). These drains are mandatory for some newer homes. The principle for the foundation drain and the French drain are the same; however, a foundation drain uses perforated PVC pipe that catches the water and diverts it around the house. Landscaping fabric is usually put on top of the PVC pipe, then gravel, then tarpaper or about 4" of straw before back filling. Make sure this is sloped properly so the water moves to a storm sewer or disposal area.

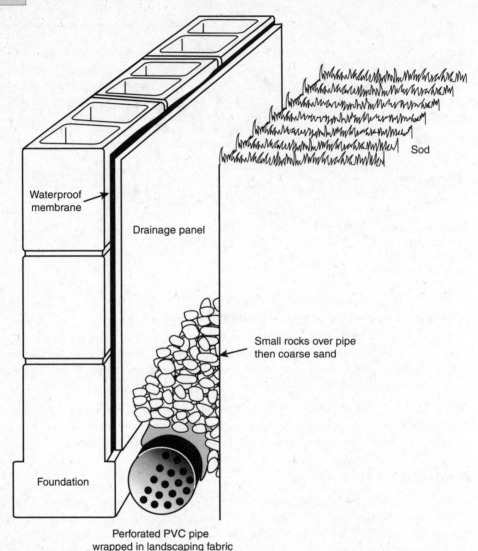

Sod

Waterproof membrane

Drainage panel

Small rocks over pipe then coarse sand

Foundation

Perforated PVC pipe wrapped in landscaping fabric

FIGURE 3.5

A foundation drain diverts water that gathers around the house.

For more information about French and foundation drains, see Chapter 6, "Drainage."

WATERPROOFING WALLS

The hydrostatic pressure on the foundation walls can break down the integrity of the concrete over time. Waterproofing the outside foundation walls is one of the best but most expensive ways to keep water from coming inside your basement. The cost to this project comes from having to dig out the area around your home to get to the walls (see Figure 3.6). Of course, you want to make sure you also install a foundation drain while you're at it. Because it is expensive, waterproofing is a fix only those with water infiltrating their basements or homes should consider.

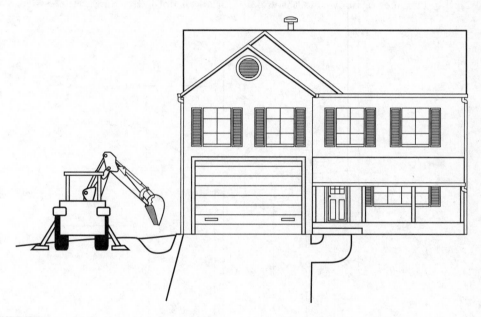

FIGURE 3.6

Excavate the soil from around your home to expose the foundation walls.

Make sure you get a product that actually "waterproofs" and not just "damp-proofs." Waterproofing is obviously better because damp-proofing products won't bridge the gap of cracks. Waterproofing products are sprayed or applied in sheets and their elasticity will bridge the gap in cracks and holes. After applying a waterproof membrane, install drainage panels attached to the outside of the foundation; this helps the water travel to the foundation drain through channels on the panels. These drainage panels have become quite popular and are now installed on the foundation walls of most new construction.

A combination of waterproofing the outside walls and foundation drains is the best way to prevent rainwater from coming into your basement.

SUMP PUMPS

A sump pump is used as a last defense against flooding. A sump pump is installed in the lowest area of a basement before water gets to the basement floor level. When the water gets to this level, the sump pump turns on and pumps out the water away from your foundation through a discharge pipe.

There are three types of sump pumps:

- **Pedestal sump pump**—This has a nonsubmergible motor that sits on the column of the pump casing above the basement floor and is not in the sump pit (see Figure 3.7).

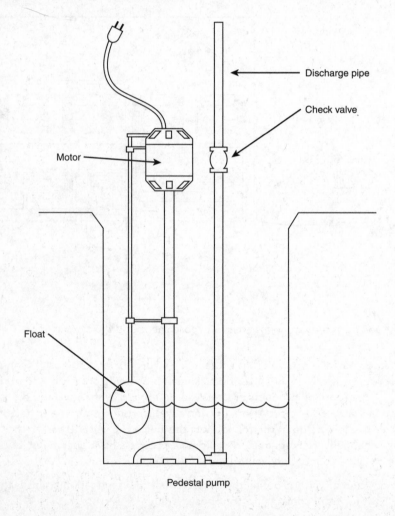

Discharge pipe

Check valve

Motor

Float

Pedestal pump

FIGURE 3.7

A pedestal sump pump.

- **Submersible sump pump**—This sits below the slab and the motor is submergible (see Figure 3.8). I like this the best since it is not seen.

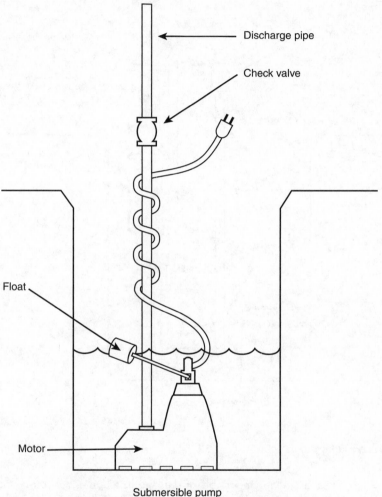

Discharge pipe

Check valve

Float

Motor

Submersible pump
(housing designed so motor can be submerged)

FIGURE 3.8

A submersible sump pump.

- **Water-powered sump pump**—This uses the city's water pressure rather than electricity (see Figure 3.9). The pump sits below the foundation and is fed by a water supply line. This type of pump cannot be installed if your house is fed by a well.

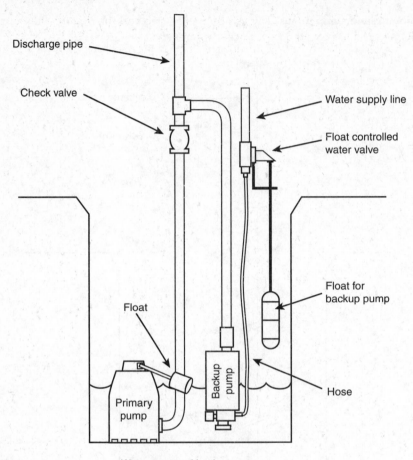

Discharge pipe

Check valve

Water supply line

Float controlled
water valve

Float for
backup pump

Float

Hose

Primary
pump

Backup
pump

Water-powered backup pump

FIGURE 3.9

A water-powered sump pump.

If the sump pump fails, it can mean lots of damage to a home, not to mention the possibility of mold. For this reason, backup pumps can be installed and are usually battery-operated or water-powered with an emergency backup alarm for when the pump goes on or if the battery is low. These are good in areas that have extreme flooding.

Common Problems

When a sump pump doesn't work properly, it is usually because it is not sized properly, not installed properly, or old and worn out; a lack of maintenance; or it's damaged from lightning or a power outage. It is important when buying a new sump pump to have the right size for your space. Know the square footage of your basement and have an idea of the depth of water that gets into your home; the professional who sells you your pump will need this information to make the best recommendation for your needs. Buy a pump that is SSPMA Certified (Sump and Sewage Pump Manufacturers Association).

> **TIP**
>
> To protect the pump from lightning, it is a good idea to have the entire house hooked up to a surge protector at the service entrance or breaker box.

Check Your Sump Pump Frequently

Do the following before the rainy season(s) to maintain your sump pump in prime working order:

- Pour water into the sump pit and make sure the pump turns on.

- Go outside to see if the water is discharging properly.

- Check to see that the float moves properly and is not restricted.

- Clean the air hole that is in the discharge line.

- Replace the battery on a backup pump every 2–3 years.

How Long Should My Sump Pump Last?

Most sump pumps have a 1- or 2-year guarantee and will last around 10 years. Of course, the life expectancy depends on how much the pump is used. Lift the lid of the tank and pour in water. Watch for the float to rise and the pump to turn on. Usually when the pump isn't working properly, the float is snagging on something. Try to reposition the float before you call in an expert.

> **NOTE**
>
> For more information about sump pumps, see the following article on State Farm Insurance's website:
>
> http://www.statefarm. com/consumer/vhouse/ articles/sumpump.htm

Sump pumps are, for the most part, inexpensive and when they do break down they usually do so on a weekend or evening when the stores are closed. You therefore might want to keep a replacement pump on hand.

CHECKLIST

❑ Check your basement for moisture or leaks by taping a piece of plastic or tin foil on the foundation wall.

❑ Remove moisture from the inside of your home.

❑ Ventilate properly.

❑ Use a dehumidifier if necessary.

❑ Check gutters and downspouts for debris and clean them when necessary.

❑ Slope your land and driveways away from your home.

❑ Install French drains and foundation drains to redirect water away from your home.

❑ Waterproof your walls.

❑ Install a sump pump in unfinished basements or under foundations to remove excess water.

DECKS AND PATIOS

4

One of my favorite construction projects is building a deck. There is something satisfying about the smell of the wood and creating more square footage off of a house. A new deck looks incredible, and if it's made out of cedar, then it smells great, too. Keeping a deck looking good requires regular maintenance.

Whether or not you stain your deck is up to you, but all decks need to be cleaned and sealed properly. Not only will you want to do this to keep your deck looking beautiful and prolong its life, but you will also want to lock in the chemicals if you have a deck made out of pressure-treated wood.

PRESSURE-TREATED WOOD

If you have a pressure-treated wooden deck that is 2 years or older, it is probably treated with chromated copper arsenate (CCA). Pressure-treated lumber was known as CCA lumber until recently, and it has a hue of green to it. The lumber industry injected chemicals into the wood using a high-pressure process—hence, the name *pressure-treated wood*. This wood has been used since the 1940s because its properties are desirable. The chemicals preserve the wood from algae and insects that normally break down untreated wood in time.

The Environmental Protection Agency (EPA) had great concerns that the CCA wood was releasing arsenic into the soil and put pressure on the manufacturers of this wood. The manufacturers of pressure-treated wood agreed to stop producing this lumber for residential use as of December 31, 2003. The lumber companies now make pressure-treated wood with ACQ (alkaline, copper, and quat) or CA (copper and azole).

Chapter 4   Decks and Patios

You want to make sure you seal a pressure-treated deck to keep the chemicals from leaking out of the wood and into the surrounding ground when it rains. There are various studies about these chemicals and how risky pressure-treated wood is to your health, but I suggest you thoroughly seal a pressure-treated deck. Just in case. For those who are really cautious, you can use a water-based epoxy sealer that spreads on like paint. It basically penetrates into the wood and encapsulates it.

CLEANING YOUR DECK

For many years, people thought it a good idea to rent a power washer and blast off the dirt from the wood. The problem with that is that it shreds the fibers of the wood on top (see Figure 4.1). To bare feet, that means splinters. I have used some mild power washers that aren't very powerful at all, and yes, you can use those, but stay clear of those heavy-duty power washers for your deck.

FIGURE 4.1

A heavy-duty power washer will shred your deck's wood.

Use an oxygen cleaner and a stiff nylon brush to clean your deck. Wet it down and then scrub the deck in the direction of the wood grain. You can rinse it off and not worry about your surrounding plants because oxygen cleaners are environmentally safe and not toxic. Once your deck is clean, wait a couple of days to make sure it is good and dry before you seal it.

How often you need to clean your deck will depend on how much use it gets, the weather, and how many trees are nearby. Use your best judgment, but definitely clean your deck once a year.

CLEANING YOUR PATIO

If you have a cement patio, you might want to rent a power washer to clean it. Whereas a power washer will hurt a wooden deck, it is fine for a cement patio. Usually, the power of the washer will be enough to clean the patio and you will not need to use a cleaner. However, if you have heavy stains, you can first make a paste of powdered detergent and water and then use a hard bristle brush to lift the stain before using the power washer.

SEALING YOUR DECK

The best way to tell if your deck needs to be sealed is to place some water directly on the deck in various places. If the water beads up and doesn't penetrate the wood, then your deck is sealed. If it soaks into the wood, you will need to seal the wood (see Figure 4.2). Usually, manufacturers suggest sealing your deck every year or two depending on the wear and tear it gets. That will be up to you to keep an eye on it.

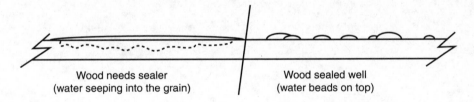

Wood needs sealer
(water seeping into the grain)

Wood sealed well
(water beads on top)

FIGURE 4.2

Water beads up on the wood if it is sealed and will seep into the wood if it is not sealed.

I recommend using synthetic resin sealers to seal your deck. These will seal the deck beautifully and will not feed the growth of algae or mildew. Oil sealers have a tendency to promote mildew and algae. This is of particular concern to those with decks that are covered by trees or shadows and do not receive an abundance of sun.

Whether you use a clear sealer or a stain/sealer, the decision is up to you. Always make sure your deck is clean and free of debris and mildew. You can use a roller, brush, sprayer, or pad to apply the coating. Be careful to not overdo it, though—less can be more. You do not want to have a build-up of sealer that will not dry or will eventually start cracking or flaking.

Before you tackle your project, make sure you check the weather forecast. Give yourself at least a day or two of sunny weather in order for the sealer or stain to dry properly.

You will have plenty of manufacturers to choose from when buying such products. Always read the directions thoroughly and apply your product exactly as recommended.

CHECKLIST

❑ Never clean a wooden deck with a high-powered pressure washer.

❑ Clean your deck at least once a year.

❑ If water absorbs into the wood of your deck, you will need to seal it.

5

Doors and Windows

Many years ago in Manhattan, I had a client who wanted to have her furniture protected from the sun and wanted bullet-resistant glass installed in her windows. It sounded like a far-fetched request until 9/11. After that day, I often thought of her and thought that maybe it wasn't such a far-fetched idea after all.

We have come a long way in the past 50 years with the types of glass we can purchase for our homes. The most important thing to look at when buying a window or door is its Energy Star label; I always suggest getting windows with Low-E glass.

There are two ways to get into a house, unless you are Santa: through the doors or through the windows. The doors and windows serve a few purposes. They allow you to keep the heat or cold on the outside, allow fresh air to enter your home, act as entryways, and allow a view.

Doors and windows are responsible for about 40% of your home's utility bill. It is important to take a look at what you can do to seal these openings and create a tighter seal in your home.

Windows

Windows are an important part in how much money you spend for your utility bill. Twenty-five percent of your home's heat can exit right through the windows. Cold air in the winter can enter through crevices and cracks around the windows, as well as through the window itself if it is not a thermal window. Condensation can occur, causing mold and rotting. Similarly, in the summer hot air can come through the same cracks and the heat from the sun can heat up your home, too. Figure 5.1 shows the ways air can get in through your windows. Having an energy-efficient window will let you be more comfortable, help to control condensation, and save you money on your utility bill. When buying a new window, make sure the window is Energy Star qualified so you know you are getting the most efficient product on the market. Energy Star is a federal standard used to rate the energy efficiency of a product, an appliance, or equipment. You want to have as much insulation as possible.

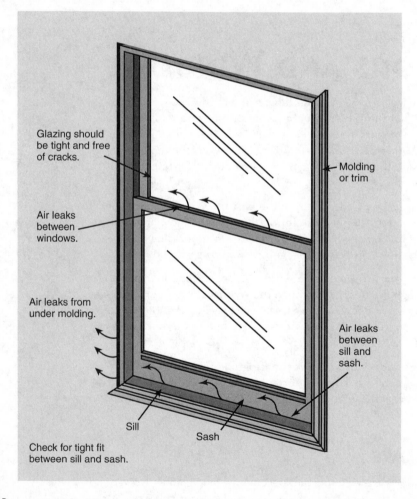

FIGURE 5.1

Ways air can get in through your windows.

If your windows are jammed, are off-kilter, or have any openings because they are not closing properly, you may need to investigate your foundation and the settling of your home. For more information on foundations, see Chapter 12, "Foundation."

Making Your Windows More Efficient

Newer homes have Energy Star–approved windows that are buttoned up tight. If you have an older home, you might have to make your windows more energy efficient.

To make your windows more energy efficient, you have the following options: repair, retrofit, reglaze, or replace.

Repair

If your window seems to be in good shape but allows air to get into your home, you can improve its air tightness by doing a few simple repairs or upgrades. Replace or adjust the sash locks if they do not properly close or tightly lock. You can also replace the hinges on casement windows. Ensure that the weather-stripping is in full contact between the frame and the sash and not interfering with the closing.

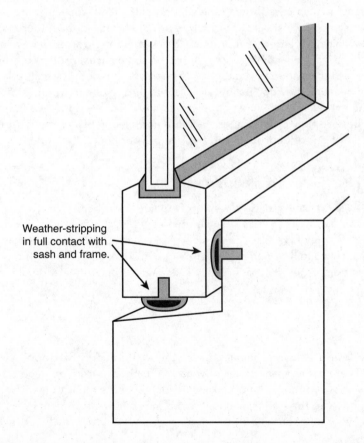

Weather-stripping in full contact with sash and frame.

FIGURE 5.2

Install weather-stripping properly so it will not interfere with the closing of the window.

Retrofit

Inspect your windows with burning incense or a piece of tissue paper to see if there is a breeze coming through the window. When you determine where the draft is coming in, then you can use weather-stripping or caulk to help seal the window.

Purchase a paintable silicone caulk and use it on any fixed joints between the trim and the wall or along the frame. I suggest putting a bead of caulk around the entire window where the trim meets the wall. Caulk any cracks or crevices and replace any cracked glazing.

Buy weather-stripping for all your doors and windows. There are various types of weather-stripping, including self-adhesive V-strip and compression.

Reglaze

Heat and cold air can pass through the window glass itself. You can increase the thermal resistance by installing interior or exterior storm windows; these will help to prevent cold air from entering your home. Storm windows trap air between the two windows, block air from coming through, and (in some cases) protect the window from storm winds. Storm windows do not help with insulation, but they can reduce your energy bill because they don't allow air to come through them. The best option is to replace the entire window with an Energy Star–qualified window. If you do install storm windows, be sure they open properly and are not fixed in place. You must have an emergency exit out of bedrooms and the rest of your home.

Plastic Film Over the Windows

A low-cost way to create a storm window is to add a plastic film over the window. There are various inexpensive films you can easily install over the front of your window. Heat-shrink film with double-sided tape is attached to the window trim and the film sticks to it. A hair dryer set on hot will make the film contract and shrink. There are other film options that use magnets or channels to hold the film in place.

Replace

If your windows are beyond repair, replace them with Energy Star–approved thermal windows. There are so many styles of windows to choose from that you can buy energy-efficient windows without compromising beauty. Take the measurements of your present window to the frame around it and bring your measurements with you when purchasing your new window.

Low-E Glass

Low-emission glass is clear glass with a microscopically thin coating. This thin film reflects heat back to its source while still allowing light to enter. In the summer, the sun's heat gets reflected back and stays outside the home; in the winter, the heat from the inside of the home is reflected back into the home and stays on the inside. Better yet, Low-E glass blocks certain amounts of UV light, which prevents fading of furniture fabric and reduces condensation on the glass. A home with properly sealed windows with Low-E glass can reduce its utility bill by up to 50%.

The two types of Low-E glass are soft coat and hard coat. The *soft coat* is a thin layer of silver sandwiched between layers of glass. The *hard coat* has tin that has been applied directly to the hot glass in its molten state. Both have pros and cons. Soft coat can be used in insulated, multipaned windows but can break down more easily. Hard coat can be used on retro-fit applications and is much sturdier, but its energy performance is slightly poorer. Low-E glass can raise the temperature of the glass on the inside to almost twice what it would be on a single pane of glass during the winter.

> **TIP**
>
> If you're buying a new window or building a room in the basement or attic, you must have an *egress window*, which is a window that a person can fit through to get out of the house in case of an emergency.

Thermal Windows

Traditional windows are single-paned (one sheet of glass). Thermal windows are either double- or triple-paned, trapping air between the layers, and are made of vinyl, metal, wood, or sometimes a combination of materials. The air is really a gas—usually argon, which acts as an excellent insulator. When buying a thermal window, check the National Fenestration Rating Council (NFRC) rating. You want a low number. The lower the score, the more the manufacturer has incorporated energy-saving features.

Locks

Windows have latches and most do not have locks. You can install window locks, but the best way to keep your home safe is by installing a security system.

DOORS

Let's face it; doors take a good bit of punishment. We are constantly going in and out of our doors, slamming them, pushing them with our feet. Between the sun, water, ice, and snow, a door takes a beating from the elements, too. Most everyone grew up with a wooden front door. Wooden doors can look great, but with all the wear and tear they suffer, they can break down prematurely. A door will swell and contract throughout the year, which is why proper maintenance is so important. Until recently, it seemed that you could either get a stylish door that wasn't energy efficient or you could get one that was well insulated but didn't look very nice. Nowadays, you can buy a door that is energy efficient *and* looks good. Manufacturers make doors out of fiberglass, wood, metal, and composites that allow your home to have great curb appeal, that keep you safe, and that have all the properties to keep the hot or cold air outside.

Much like windows, doors need to be sealed tight with proper weather-stripping and caulking to seal the cracks. You can buy doors *pre-hung*, which means they have the entire entry system all together: door, jamb, and hinges. This is a good idea so that the entire operating system is made together, ensuring a more buttoned-up entry door (see Figure 5.3).

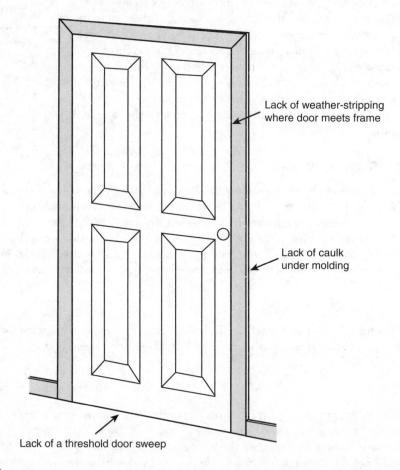

Lack of weather-stripping where door meets frame

Lack of caulk under molding

Lack of a threshold door sweep

FIGURE 5.3

Air can escape from or come into your home around your door if it is not properly sealed.

Types of Doors

Wood doors are the nicest-looking doors. They come in various types of woods that can be stained and sealed beautifully. There are also basic paint-grade doors that are made to be painted; therefore, the door is made of less-expensive wood and is cheaper. You will need to keep an eye on your front door to check if it needs another coat of paint or polyurethane since wood doors are highly susceptible to moisture and sun damage.

Fiberglass doors are very durable and practically maintenance free. Usually they have longer warranties than wooden doors. The frames are made of wood and encapsulated in fiberglass. Fiberglass doors are usually less expensive than wood doors, too.

Composite doors are usually made of fiberglass and a composite. These doors can look exactly like a wood door. In my opinion, these are superior doors since you do not have to worry about warping or outside elements and they carry a long warranty. Sometimes these doors can be as expensive as wooden doors, but they outlast wooden doors and are well worth the money.

Steel doors are perfect if you are looking for security. These doors are the strongest and won't warp or crack. The damage to these doors comes in the form of dents, which can be repaired with some auto bonding.

French doors are made of glass and usually wood or a composite. Much like the other doors described, you will want to make sure these doors are sealed well and have the Energy Star rating.

Sliding glass doors turn a huge space into a see-through wall. It is important to buy new glass doors with Low-E glass and UV protection since they allow an enormous amount of light in. Always keep the tracks clean to keep them in good working order. Graphite can be sprinkled in the bottom track to keep the doors sliding smoothly.

Interior doors are not as expensive as other doors because they are only used for privacy. There are hundreds of types to choose from and a range of prices to fit your budget.

Storm Doors

Storm doors usually have a pane that can be changed from a window to a screen. These doors are supposed to reduce air leaking into your front or back door in the winter, yet allow fresh air to come in through the screen in the summer. Storm doors are made of wood, steel, or aluminum.

Locks

Key-in-the-knob locks are virtually useless when protecting your home from burglars. Double-cylinder deadbolts are the most secure locks because they require a key on either side to unlock them. However, they also pose a hazard if you're trying to get out of your home and you can't find the key. For this reason, I suggest a panic-proof deadbolt that has a thumb latch to operate the deadbolt from the inside.

Make sure the deadbolt extends at least 1" out from the edge of the door. The *strike plate* is the plate on the jamb of the door that the deadbolt extends into, and it should be screwed in with screws long enough to reach the studs behind the doorframe.

There is various hardware you can find to lock a sliding glass door. A simple way is to close the door and then drill up at the top of both glass doors, directly through both doors and using a pin or common nail to go through the holes of both doors. You can also cut a piece of wood or metal to fit behind the one door.

I don't suggest having French doors for a front door since they are easy to break into. Get a heavy-duty vertical bolt to keep the stationary door in place.

The best way to keep your home safe is to install a deadbolt lock and a security system.

CHECKLIST

❑ Do what you can to seal around your doors and windows.

❑ Always look for an Energy Star rating when buying a window or door.

❑ Always get windows with Low-E glass.

❑ Install a deadbolt lock for your entry doors.

6

DRAINAGE

I feel fortunate to have grown up in the South where storms had lightning and thunder. Once, my brother and I were gazing out the window counting the time between flash and sound when we saw a tree across the street get struck by lightning and sizzle in front of our eyes. In a big storm, not only were the lightning and thunder dramatic, but so was the water. The creek behind our house would get higher and higher, threatening our thresholds on an hourly basis.

When I was about 10 years old, I remember my father and our next door neighbor, Wallace, spending about three weekends putting in a surface drainage system. Basically, it was a long ditch lined with bricks to channel the water away from our respective homes. It seemed to do the trick, and for many years our basement stayed fairly dry during these storms.

CATCHING RAINWATER

After reading Chapter 3, "Basements," you know how important it is to drain water away from the house. The first line of defense is through a gutter system that should be pitched at a slight angle to direct the rainwater into a downspout and then guide the water either above ground or below ground at least 10 feet away from the home. In areas with heavy rainfall, the downspouts are tied into a catch basin. These catch basins then carry the water in a solid drainpipe to a drywell.

Chapter 6	Drainage

For houses without gutters, a drainage system, much like the foundation drain, should be installed at the roof's drip line around the house and lead into a drywell or an outlet pipe (see Figure 6.1). This is similar to a modern-day French drain, which I get into more specifically later in this chapter.

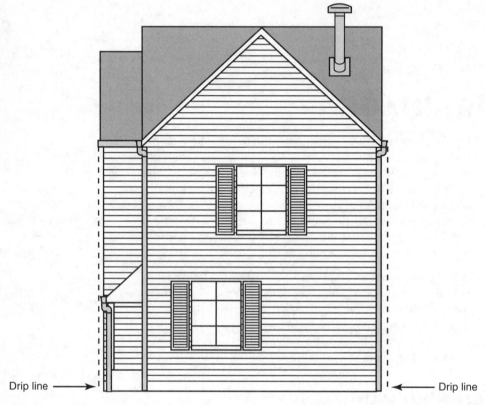

Drip line ⟶   ⟵ Drip line

FIGURE 6.1

The roof's drip line.

Having the proper drainage system for your home's landscaping is a necessity for keeping a dry home, but it is also important for your plants. Just as important as proper irrigation is for your lawn, you also need to remove excess water so it won't kill sensitive plants or trees. Ground that was once frozen receives a deluge of water come springtime. If the lawn is improperly graded, rainwater can puddle up and suffocate plants. In most cases, once the water has done damage to your yard, it will find ways to enter your home through cracks in the foundation. When enough water builds up against the foundation wall, this is called *hydrostatic pressure*, and it can surely crack the foundation and cause seepage into your home.

Always check with a landscape designer about the proper way to divert the water on your grounds. Sometimes it may mean regrading the land by either removing soil or hauling in more soil to take up low spots. Your landscape specialist will be able to tell you whether you will need drains to help you remove rainwater. However, before you drain the water into the street or a sewer drain, make sure you check with local codes.

There are two types of drainage systems: surface and sub-surface drainage.

SURFACE DRAINAGE

A *surface drainage* system collects excess water from planter beds; turf areas; and hardscaping such as driveways, walkways, and swimming pools and works well in areas where the soil is made of clay. The water flows to a catch basin that collects the debris before it can enter the drainage pipes (see Figure 6.2). The most typical surface system is a shallow trench. These open trenches are very effective in removing excess water quickly from the landscape into a catch basin.

> **NOTE**
>
> Older drywells were made of a 55-gallon oil drums that had holes punched in them, leaving them open for rust and decay. Today, most landscapers install a plastic drywell or a concrete drywell for large volumes of water.

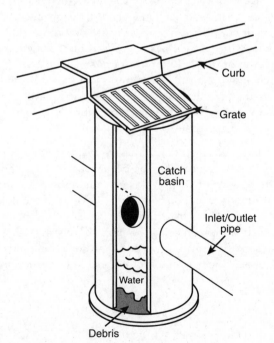

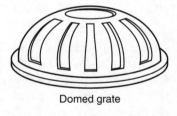

Domed grate

FIGURE 6.2

The surface drainage system collects excess water that flows into a catch basin.

Sometimes water is caught through a grate attached to a nonperforated pipe leading to a catch basin. A few types of grates are used to catch the water. *Round* drainage grates are typically used in grassy or turf areas. *Square* drainage grates are used in parking lots, driveways, walkways, swimming pools, and most hardscaped areas. *Domed* grates or atrium drainage grates have a little dome-like cage that prevents debris from building up on top of the grate. These are used in areas such as window wells and planting areas with stone, bark, mulch, or various landscaping materials that could potentially clog up a drain.

Channel drains are another form of surface drainage that collect water through an extended trough and are covered by a long grate. Typically, these drains are used in paved areas.

The catch basin and the pipes carrying the water all need to be large enough to handle the anticipated volume of water. It's always better to go bigger than smaller. Most people use solid 4" or 6" PVC drain pipes for removing excess surface water.

SUBSURFACE DRAINAGE

Subsurface drains are used in areas with high silt or sand content. The most popular type of drain used in subsurface drainage is the French drain (see Figure 6.3). This was named after a farmer and judge, Henry French, who lived in Concord, Massachusetts, in the mid-1800s. A true French drain is a drain without a pipe. Originally, a French drain was a trench that was dug about 12" below the surface of the ground and 2' around the perimeter of the cellar. Tile was laid at the bottom and then bark or small rocks were laid on top of the tile. This would catch and divert the water away from the cellar and into an outlet drain. As things changed, the French drain was then made of gravel wrapped in landscape fabric to keep out any debris. On top of this tube of gravel is either more gravel or a layer of coarse sand and then sod to finish it off.

Nowadays, many landscape designers use a more modern drainage system with a perforated pipe and also call it a French drain (see Figure 6.4). The perforated pipe is used in foundation drains as well. Similar to the French drain, gravel is placed on the bottom a few inches deep; then a 4"–6" perforated pipe is laid on top of this gravel with the holes facing down. The perforated pipe is covered with a filter fabric or landscape fabric that allows only water to enter and keeps debris from entering the pipe. More gravel is placed on top of the pipe with coarse sand or straw on top, and then sod. The depth of your drainage can range from 8" to 3' deep. Check with a professional as to how deep your drainage should be.

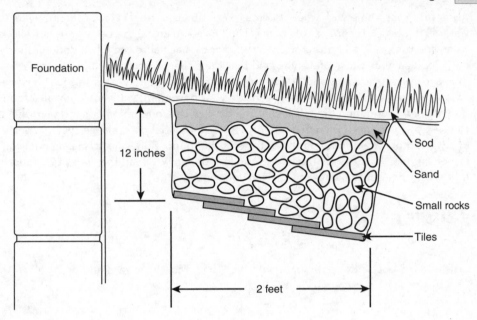

FIGURE 6.3

An original French drain does not have a pipe.

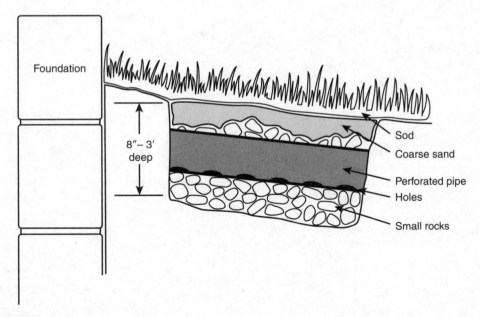

FIGURE 6.4

The modern version of a French drain has a perforated pipe.

Chapter 6 Drainage

Always do your homework when it comes to troubleshooting water problems since water is the biggest menace to a home. The more you know, the better off you will be when speaking with a contractor or landscaper to make sure the job is done properly. Be sure you check their references and that their clients are happy because most drainage systems are guaranteed for only a year. You definitely want this job to last you as long as possible. If water is getting inside your basement, you should install a foundation drain. A foundation drain is laid at the base of the foundation and installed the same way as a modern French drain. An effective foundation drainage system consists of a waterproof membrane on the outside of the foundation wall; drainage panels on top of this membrane and attached to the foundation wall lead the water to a foundation drain to direct the water away from your home.

CHECKLIST

❑ Check the grading around your home.

❑ Hire a landscape designer and contractor to regrade your yard and/or install a drainage system if needed.

7

Driveways

I remember the driveway I grew up on quite well. Most people don't take notice to such detail unless they are learning how to roller skate or skateboard like I did when I was a kid. You see, it is very important to know exactly where the cracks are in the driveway so you pick up your body weight when going over them. It took me a couple of wrong moves and a nice face plant on cement to learn the location of those expansion joints! Of course, I didn't understand the expansion joint concept when I was a kid. I just thought we couldn't afford a whole driveway delivered in one piece. I hadn't a clue that it was poured.

Driveway Components

We often here the term *curb appeal,* which means how the home looks from the curb or street. There are many contributing factors to this, one of which is the driveway. Various types of driveways are distinguished by the materials used to make them: asphalt; concrete; brick; thick stone blocks or manmade pavers; and loose materials such as gravel, pine needles, wood chips, and seashells. Both asphalt and concrete driveways need to be sealed periodically.

No matter what type of driveway material you choose, it is important to properly slope it for proper drainage and to ensure water doesn't puddle and freeze on the driveway, causing cracks. The slope should be a 1/4" running foot pitched away from the home (see Figure 7.1). This means that, for every 12", the driveway gradually slopes down 1/4". If you were to take a level across a 20' driveway, the end of the driveway would be 5" below the grade of the beginning of the driveway where it meets the house.

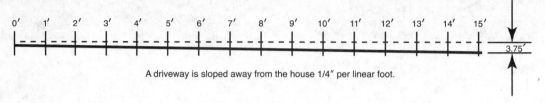

A driveway is sloped away from the house 1/4" per linear foot.

FIGURE 7.1

Driveway should gradually slope down 1/4" for every linear foot.

The subgrade of the driveway is very important when using asphalt or concrete. The area you live in will determine the thickness of the subgrade. Remember, you want your driveway to be evenly poured if it is 4" thick concrete and evenly laid if it is asphalt.

Asphalt

Asphalt is one of the most popular materials for driveways since it is fairly inexpensive and holds up well in cold weather, making it easy to remove snow from it. Asphalt is made of black hot tar that is poured on top of a prepared bed. This is what covers most streets. If you find your asphalt driveway has cracks, address the issue immediately. If water freezes in the cracks, it will widen the cracks and let water get in underneath. Not only will it start to look bad, but you will eventually deal with weeds growing up through the cracks and the integrity will be compromised. You need to fill cracks and patch any holes before you seal the driveway.

Concrete

Concrete driveways are more expensive than asphalt but are very popular in severe winter areas since they hold up quite well in freezing conditions. Concrete is made of cement, aggregate (crushed stone), water, and additives. Concrete can be brushed, stained, embedded with stone, or molded (which also makes it popular).

Because concrete is a denser material than asphalt, it needs to have joints to expand. A 4" thick pad of concrete should have an expansion joint for every 8'–12' of length. The joint should be 1" deep. If the joints are too far apart, the concrete will start to crack over time. These joints are filled with rubber, cork, fiber, or foam filler and can be replaced if they break down over time.

Brick or Pavers

Brick is used to give an old-fashioned or antique look to the driveway. Brick comes in various warm tones and colors to give your curb appeal a textured look. The nice feature with brick is that you can lay it in different patterns, creating a pleasing effect. If a brick is broken or cracked, it's easy to remove and replace it. Artificial stone pavers are less expensive than brick and offer the same ease of replacing a broken paver. These thick pavers can be made out of various cementous materials offering different patterns and colors.

Brick is usually placed in a bed of sand that has been tampered in place. Once the brick has been laid, loose sand is then brushed across the cracks to fill up the gaps. You should ask the company who sells you the brick whether you will need to seal them and, if so, how often. Again, pay attention to the slope of the driveway to let water drain properly.

Stone Blocks

Stone blocks are considered high-end driveway materials because you must use dense stone such as granite to handle the load of cars. This can be quite expensive. Companies are making concrete blocks to look like large stones to save on costs. The patterns can create a rich texture for your driveway.

Loose Materials

In areas that are not concerned with snow or freezing weather, loose materials such as pine straw, wood chips, gravel, and seashells are a great low-maintenance option. Always use materials that are native to your area since you will need to keep refilling areas as time goes by. Obviously, you will not need to seal loose materials.

Sealing Your Driveway

It is important to seal your driveway to keep it in good shape and to prevent water from getting through the cracks and compromising the strength of the base. Before sealing the driveway, remove all debris and oil stains. There are some fantastic, environmentally friendly products on the market to remove stains, but these can be rather expensive. You may want to try removing the stains by using some powder detergent with a little water to make a paste and a hard bristle brush and then rinsing thoroughly. For stubborn stains, I recommend using a power washer. This will get your driveway looking like new. After cleaning, cut back the grass around the edges and make sure you let it dry properly before sealing.

Another thing you need to do before sealing your driveway is inspect your driveway for cracks. Any cracks that are more than 1/8" wide will need to be filled. You can find an assortment of crack fillers at your hardware store. Some are liquid that are squeezed through a bottle, and other fillers come in a caulk-like tube (see Figure 7.2).

Chapter 7 Driveways

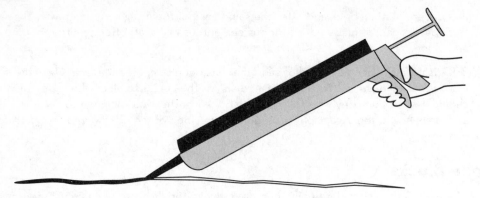

FIGURE 7.2

Fill cracks with caulk.

Make sure you buy the right crack filler for the type of driveway you have. If you have a wide crack or hole, you might need to buy a bag of patching material or aggregate filler, also known as a *cold patch*.

An asphalt driveway should be sealed 6 months after it has been poured (you need to let it cure before sealing). Then you'll need to reseal it every 1–3 years thereafter, depending on your climate. Concrete driveways can be sealed after installation and after they have cured. Make sure your contractor comes back to seal your driveway; it is part of their job. A concrete driveway should be sealed every 3–5 years. The months between March and October have the best temperatures for sealing your driveway.

> **TIP**
>
> Always check your weather forecast before sealing your driveway. You want to have a few hot and dry days after applying the sealant.

When sealing your driveway, wear clothing you don't mind ruining because this can be messy. Also, protect your body and eyes. Buy the proper sealant for your driveway and spread it on with an applicator, like the one shown in Figure 7.3. One side will be a squeegee to smooth the sealer over the driveway, and the other side will be a brush to push the sealer into cracks no bigger than 1/8". (A crack any bigger needs to be filled.)

Most concrete sealers are clear but some have color or glitter in them. Asphalt driveways have the option to use a black and thick resurfacer that can last up to 6 years depending on the product. This is spread over a clean asphalt driveway and will fill in cracks 1/8" wide and deep. Some products give excellent traction as well. Always follow manufacturer's directions.

The length of time your driveway will last depends on the care you give it and the climate you live in. The average life span of asphalt is around 10 years. The average life of a concrete or brick driveway is roughly 24 years.

FIGURE 7.3

Use an applicator to apply the sealant.

CHECKLIST

❑ Properly slope your driveway 1/4" per foot for proper drainage if pouring a new driveway.

❑ Refill bald areas in your driveway if using loose materials.

❑ Fill cracks that are wider than 1/8".

❑ Replace filler in concrete joints.

❑ Properly seal your driveway to extend its life and to keep water from compromising the subgrade.

8

ELECTRICITY

For those of you who are a little squeamish about working with electricity, I have a confession: I am, too. Well, at least I used to be more than I am now. I understand how electricity works, but I guess because I can't really see it like I can see water running through a pipe, it unnerves me a bit. Electricity is a complete miracle in my opinion. We are all controlled by it. It is an electrical pulse from our brain that makes our heart beat and our organs and muscles work properly. Yet it is an electrical current that makes so many things in our homes work, too. No matter how many times I write about it, I am still in utter awe of its power!

GETTING ELECTRICITY TO YOUR HOME

Electricity comes to your home through a system called the *power distribution grid* (see Figure 8.1). Electricity originates at the power plant. Each power plant has a large spinning electrical generator, yet something needs to spin it. Hydropower plants use a dam and water to spin the generator. When harnessing water isn't an option, a steam turbine is used. Oil, gas, coal, or nuclear energy is typically used create the steam to spin the generator. Once the electricity is harnessed, it then goes to the power substation to decrease, or *step-down*, the voltage of the electricity for distribution.

Electricity comes in alternating current (AC) or direct current (DC). The power plant produces alternating current that comes to your home as single-phase power. Miles of wires are either buried or strung on power lines to bring this electricity into your home, depending on whether you live in an urban area, a suburb, or a rural area.

Chapter 8 | Electricity

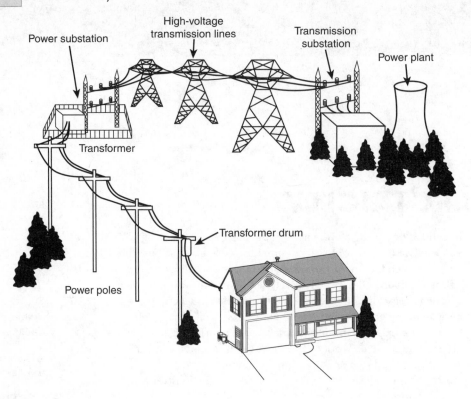

FIGURE 8.1

Power distribution grid.

If you have a telephone pole that distributes electricity to your neighborhood, take a look at the wires coming into your home from the pole. There are three wires that feed into your home. Two wires coming from the transformer are both insulated and carry 120 volts of electricity, bringing in a total of 240 volts into your home. Both of these wires enter through a watt-hour meter that allows the power company to keep track of the amount of electricity you use. The third wire is usually not insulated and is called the *ground wire*.

The following are definitions of some electrical terms:

- **Volts**—The pressure pushing electrons along in an electrical circuit is called the *voltage*, and it is measured in *volts*. A typical outlet has 120 volts running through it.

- **Amps**—The number of electrons that are moving in an electrical circuit is called the *current* or the *amperage*, and it is measured in *amps*.

- **Watts**—The standard measurement of electricity, which the utility company uses to charge you for your usage. The number of amps multiplied by the number of volts determines watts. The voltage coming from your wall outlet is 120 volts. If you have an appliance that is 10 amps, you multiply amps by volts: 10 × 120 = 1200. So, you have a 1200-watt appliance.

- **Kilowatt**—A *kilowatt* is 1,000 watts. If something is 1200 watts, it is 1.2 kilowatts.

The most common mistakes when working with electricity are

- Not turning off the power at the breaker panel

- Not making a plan before tackling the job

- Overloading circuits by plugging in too many electronics or appliances

- Not labeling the circuit breakers at the panel

- Not using the proper junction box for wiring

- Using improper wiring to the terminals

- Not mounting the switches and outlets properly (all should be flush to the face of the wall)

- Not using UL-approved materials

- Not having nail guards

- Not using proper weatherproof boxes for outdoor outlets and fixtures

- Not having your work inspected

- Not following local code

Be **VERY** careful when working with electricity. It's best to call a professional electrician if you are having any problems.

POWER OUTAGE

If yous have experienced a power outage, you will understand the importance of a generator. A couple days without electricity can be costly since the food in your refrigerator and freezer will go bad and need to be thrown away. You will be prepared for such an unfortunate turn of events if you have a generator.

Determine how much power you will need before purchasing a generator. You may need to get an electrician to help you with this. I recommend you not hook up the generator directly to your home's wiring because the amperage to operate your home is greater than the power of the generator. Instead, connect the

TIP

Always have a corded phone to use in case of a power outage. Most times when there is a blackout, the telephone lines still emit enough electricity for a corded phone to work. Conversely, a cordless phone will not work because it needs electricity for the base to communicate with the phone.

appliances and machines that you want to operate directly to the outlets on the generator. A generator needs to be stored outside so the fumes can dissipate outside and not in your home.

FUSE BOX OR CIRCUIT BREAKER

The two insulated wires carrying 120 volts each pass through the watt-hour meter and enter the circuit breaker box or the fuse box. These are both set up for safety reasons.

The following scenarios can blow a fuse or trip a switch in a circuit breaker:

- Too many appliances or machines running at the same time, overloading the circuit

- A mouse eating through a wire connecting the power to the ground

- A vacuum or hairdryer overheating, causing a connection between the power and the ground

- A loose wire in an outlet or a lamp that connects it directly through the ground

- Hanging something on the wall and nailing or screwing right through an electrical wire, causing the power to go directly to the ground

If you have any of these types of scenarios and you have a **fuse box**, the overload of power creates an enormous amount of heat. This heat runs through the wire and through the fuse, causing the foil or wire in the fuse to vaporize. This immediately cuts off electrical flow to the outlets and switches off that circuit. You need to fix the problem and then replace the fuse. A **circuit breaker** works much the same way: The heat trips the circuit breaker, causing an immediate stoppage of electrical flow to that circuit. This shuts off all lights, outlets, and switches that run on that circuit. A circuit breaker box has several switches that go to various locations of your home. It also has a main breaker to cut off the power to your entire house.

> **TIP**
>
> Make sure you know where your fuse box or circuit breaker box is located. Always keep a flashlight with working batteries nearby.

> **TIP**
>
> Whether you have a fuse box or circuit breaker box, it's a good idea to identify and label the areas of your home that connect to various fuses or circuits (see Figure 8.2).

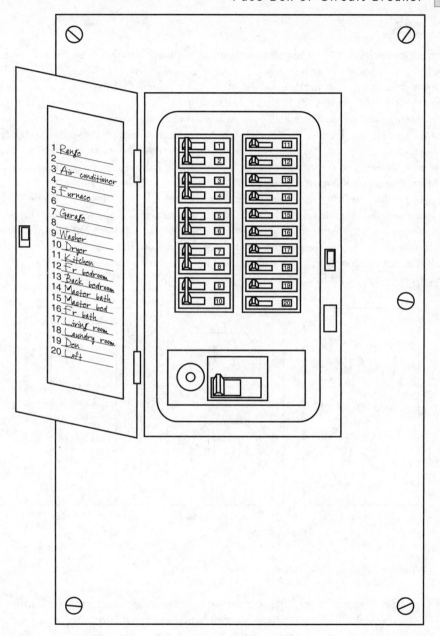

FIGURE 8.2

Circuit breaker box with breakers labeled to identify the corresponding areas of the home.

OUTLETS

You probably have two-pronged, ungrounded outlets if you live in an older home. Outlets, also known as *receptacles*, can wear out over time from repeated use. This deterioration can wear out the plastic faceplate or the outlet itself. If the prongs of the plug bridge the electrical contacts, an intense electrical arcing can cause fire, electrical shock, and even burns. Check all your outlets for damage and deterioration and replace them immediately if they're worn out. Changing from an ungrounded electrical system to a grounded electrical system requires running a ground wire throughout the home and connecting it to every outlet, switch, and electrical fixture. It also requires new outlet boxes and installing new three-prong outlets. If you have the budget, I definitely suggest upgrading your home's electrical system because it will bring your home up to the present safety standards. Because this requires a professional and can be rather expensive, there are other options you might consider. Replacing damaged two-prong outlets with new two-prong outlets is the least favorable option, but it at least ensures that the outlet is not worn out. In this case, you will need to buy an adapter that fits on your three-prong cord and fits into the two-prong outlet.

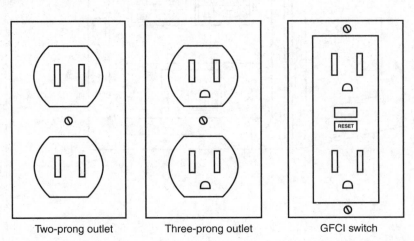

Two-prong outlet   Three-prong outlet   GFCI switch

FIGURE 8.3

A two-prong outlet, three-prong outlet, and GFCI switch.

The next best option to rewiring your home is to install ground fault circuit interrupters (GFCI) outlets. A GFCI outlet turns your receptacle from a two-prong to a three-prong outlet and has a mini breaker within the outlet. If something overheats the outlet, the interior breaker trips and cuts off the power to the outlet.

After 1993, building codes began requiring GFCI outlets to be installed within 6 feet of all wet locations, such as bathrooms, kitchens, and garages. Personally, I prefer all the switches in kitchens and baths to have GFCI outlets.

Local Codes

When adding on a room, always check your local codes. Contact your state's Building Inspector's Association or check with the building inspector at your county's building department or courthouse to obtain a copy of the local building codes.

> ## Caution
> Always turn off the circuit breaker in the circuit breaker box that corresponds to the outlet or light switch you are working on.

Although every area is governed by different codes, most codes require outlets to be spaced every 12 feet or less on the same wall. Keep the outlets at the same height and install a light switch at each entrance to the room. The National Electrical Code requires all residential homes to use No. 12 gauge wire for electrical wiring.

Outdoor Wiring

Ground fault interrupters (GFIs) are required in all outdoor fixtures and wiring. These electronic devices cut the power immediately if they detect a current to ground that exceeds a predetermined value.

There are two types of cable: UF and TW. UF is covered in heavy plastic sheathing that acts as insulation to the wire. This wire or cable is designed to be placed in the ground without being protected in a metal conduit. TW wire has a thin thermoplastic insulation to protect it from moisture and is then encased in a protective metal conduit.

Switch and outlet boxes should be made of heavy cast metal when mounted outdoors. The cover plates should also be made of the same heavy cast metal and outfitted with weatherproof gaskets.

Outdoor light fixtures use the same characteristics as the outlet boxes. Again, there is a gasket to seal the joint between the fixture box and the cover.

You can use three kinds of conduit: rigid aluminum, rigid steel, and rigid plastic. Rigid aluminum is easier to work with than rigid steel, but it must be coated with bituminous paint when buried in concrete to prevent it from corroding. PVC (polyvinyl chloride) is normally used above ground, and high-density polyethylene is used underground. PVC should be painted with two coats of latex paint to prevent any deterioration from direct sunlight. When digging a trench for your cables, you will probably have to dig at least 18", although I prefer at least a 24" depth for UF cable and possibly less for rigid metal or plastic conduit. Again, always check the local building codes for depth.

Light Bulbs

If you have visited a home center recently, you may have noticed the plethora of light bulbs. It used to be that there was just one kind of light bulb with different wattages, depending on how bright you wanted the light to be. However nowadays, there are so many to choose from, it's easy to get overwhelmed.

Knowing the following bulb terminology will help you choose the right bulb for your needs:

- **Watts**—As mentioned earlier, watts are the standard unit of measure of electricity. The higher the wattage, the brighter the bulb.

- **Lumens**—Standard measure of light. A 100-watt bulb produces about 1600 lumens.

- **Incandescent**—This is a typical light bulb that has a filament that is heated when turned on. This filament glows, producing the bulb's light. A *halogen* light bulb is an incandescent bulb with a few modifications: one being halogen gas in the bulb. These bulbs are smaller and can burn very brightly, last longer, and use less energy than a standard incandescent bulb.

- **Fluorescent**—Type of light bulb or tube filled with a mercury vapor. Ultraviolet light is emitted when electricity flows through it. The coating on the inside of the bulb or tube is what turns the ultraviolet rays into visible light.

- **Life**—This is the lifespan of the bulb estimated in the number of hours the bulb will stay lit.

Tip

Always use weatherproof bulbs outside. They will resist shattering when the temperature drops.

Light bulbs come in various colors for mood lighting or to mimic natural lighting. Three-way light bulbs are for fixtures that allow for three different light settings.

The most energy-efficient of all the light bulbs is the compact fluorescent bulb (CFL). This type of bulb uses 67% less energy than standard incandescent bulbs and therefore lasts longer.

Dimmers

There is nothing like being able to create an instant mood with the touch of a button. For this reason, dimmers are an excellent choice. If you buy an inexpensive dimmer switch, you may hear a buzzing sound coming from your light bulb—this buzzing sound is the filament in an incandescent light bulb. A more expensive dimmer switch has components in it to store the electrical charge that makes the filament buzz.

If you are buying a dimmer for a ceiling fan, always make sure you buy a dimmer specifically for a ceiling fan. Never use a regular dimmer for this purpose.

SURGE PROTECTORS

Surge protectors are used to protect your electronic devices from *power surges*, or increases in the voltage that normally flows into your home. As discussed earlier, the standard voltage in household wiring is 120 volts. If the voltage rises above 120 volts, the pressure of the higher volts can ruin electronic equipment or machinery.

A typical scenario is in the summer when you're operating high-powered electrical devices such as air conditioners and refrigerators. The compressors and motors require a great deal of energy to turn such devices on and off. This switching creates a demand for power that in turn upsets the steady flow of voltage. Often when these machines turn off, the surge in power goes directly to delicate equipment, such as computers, televisions, stereos, and microwaves.

A standard strip surge protector passes the 120 volts of electrical current from the outlet to the electrical devices plugged into the power strip. If there is a spike or surge of electricity (volts), the surge protector diverts the extra volts into the outlet's grounding wire. A surge protector acts as a pressure relief valve to your electronics.

I am a big believer in buying a whole house surge protector that is installed at the breaker box and protects your entire home's electrical equipment. Hire a licensed electrician to install this for you.

CHECKLIST

- ❑ Know where your fuse box or circuit breaker is and have extra fuses on hand.
- ❑ Keep a flashlight near the fuse box.
- ❑ Buy a generator in case of a power outage.
- ❑ Keep a corded phone handy in case of a power outage.
- ❑ Upgrade your electrical system if you have ungrounded, two-prong outlets.
- ❑ Use GFCI outlets in kitchens, in bathrooms, and outside.
- ❑ Always check your local codes when installing new wiring in your home.
- ❑ Use the proper wire or cable when running electricity outside.
- ❑ Buy the proper dimmer for a ceiling fan or light fixture.
- ❑ Use a surge protector to protect your electronics and sensitive appliances.

9

EXTERIOR MAINTENANCE

I grew up in a ranch home with brick and clapboard siding as the exterior materials. The bricks required no maintenance aside from washing them. The clapboard siding and shutters needed painting only every 10–15 years. My folks were good about not letting the paint get to the point of peeling and allowing water to damage the wood. The biggest part of the job, as I recall, was the prep work. The sanding, caulking, and priming were the most laborious parts of the job, but it is that very prep work that ensures a paint job that will last years and years.

YOUR HOME'S EXTERIOR

The exterior of your home takes a good bit of wear and tear from the sun's ultraviolet rays and whatever is dropping from the sky: rain, sleet, snow, or hail. Moisture is one of the biggest enemies to your home because it produces mildew and eventually breaks down the many building materials used to construct it.

Every home has an exterior layer that gives it curb appeal and protects its structural framework from the elements. There are various materials to choose from, depending on style and climate, such as clapboard, wood shingles, metal or vinyl siding, brick, and stucco.

Below the exterior layer is the *sheathing*. When a home is framed and insulated, the sheathing is nailed to the studs on the outside of the frame to give structural support and also to act as a substrate to which to attach the exterior layer or siding. Sheathing types include oriented strand board (OSB), wafer board, and plywood. After the sheathing is installed, house wrap is applied and then the exterior protection (such as siding) is installed. *House wrap* is a fabric-like material that lets moisture pass through but stops air.

SIDING

Siding is an exterior wall covering that protects a home from moisture, heat, and wind. There are various types and styles to choose from, such as solid wood, shingles, fiberboard, plywood, fiber-cement, metal or vinyl siding, stucco, brick, and stone. The most traditional form of wood siding is made from solid wood; however, as solid wood siding became more expensive, manufacturers engineered less expensive options to look like solid wood, such as wood composites, cement, vinyl, aluminum, and steel.

It is important to install house wrap or building felt before siding is installed since siding will not seal out all moisture or wind. Siding is installed from the bottom, overlapping the bottom panel. The trim openings around the windows and doors must also overlap so the water runs off the trim and siding and not behind it. Caulking is also an important step when using wood and fiber-cement boards to seal gaps and cracks around doors and windows.

Wood Siding

Solid wood siding is beautiful, strong, and timeless. It can be installed horizontally, vertically, or diagonally. An advantage of wood siding is that you can stain or paint it. There are disadvantages, to wood, though: Solid wood is expensive, needs to be painted regularly with a good bit of prep work, and is susceptible to rot and termites. Traditional solid wood siding was often made of cedar or redwood because those woods are resistant to decay. However, cedar and redwood are very expensive, so ponderosa pine, cypress, Douglas fir, and larch are now more commonly used for wood siding. You should use a clear sealer for prime-quality grades of lumber and stain or paint the other types.

Wood siding is also known as *clapboards* or *plank siding* and is usually installed horizontally and overlapped in various ways: plain bevel, rabbited bevel, shiplap, or tongue and groove (see Figure 9.1).

Replacing a damaged board is fairly easy since it can be cut to fit the damaged piece. Matching the color requires simply painting the board the same color as the rest of the siding. This is true for all the types of wood siding.

You will need to paint the exterior of your home about every 8 years. This figure can change depending on the exposure to the sun and the extreme elements that may hit your siding. Always make sure you clean the wood siding and let it dry before painting. Then, remove any flaking paint chips and repair and caulk any cracks, gaps, or gouges. Sand the siding smoothly and prime it when necessary—always prime bare wood.

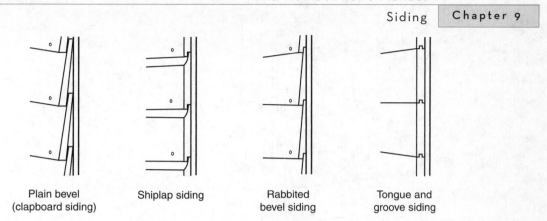

Plain bevel
(clapboard siding)

Shiplap siding

Rabbited
bevel siding

Tongue and
groove siding

FIGURE 9.1

The types of clapboard or plank siding are plain bevel, shiplap, rabbited bevel, and tongue and groove.

There are many types of paints you can use. Years ago, people only painted with oil-based paints, and many people today think that is the only way to go. I personally am not a big fan of oil-based paint for home exteriors since it can be messy, is hard to clean, and requires a caustic solvent when cleaning brushes. Because there are so many great latex paints, I suggest an exterior latex acrylic paint that is durable and allows the paint to expand and contract with the temperature. You can use a latex paint over oil paint, but you cannot use an oil paint over latex paint without priming it first with a primer specifically to be applied over latex allowing an oil paint on top of it.

Remember to cut back bushes and vegetation around your home to make it easier to paint and position your ladder.

> **TIP**
>
> Pour a mildew-resistant additive into your paint unless your paint already has one in it.

Wood Shingles

Wood shingles are another form of wood siding used on contemporary and Victorian homes. This is a popular look for cabins because the shingles, also known as *shakes*, can give a home a rustic look and blend well with the landscape. Most of these shingles are made of cedar, which lasts up to 30 years. Shingles are installed from the ground up, and the seams are staggered with the overlapping shingle above it to ensure water doesn't channel its way behind them (see Figure 9.2). Cedar shingles do need restaining every 5 years, but if you paint them, they may hold up for 8 years before needing a fresh coat. If your home is in a humid climate, treat the shingles with a mildew control in the stain or paint.

Chapter 9 | Exterior Maintenance

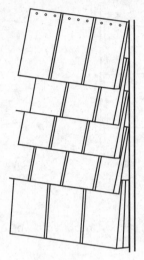

The first row of shingles completely covers
the starter row. Joints do not line up.

FIGURE 9.2

Wood shingles overlap the bottom shingle, causing the joints to not line up.

Fiberboard Siding

Fiberboard siding is a compression of wood fibers and glue that comes in various widths and lengths. It is popular because it has the look and feel of real wood minus the expense, it can be purchased already primed so it is ready to paint, and it usually is guaranteed against termites and rot. The disadvantages are similar to wood siding in the respect that fiberboard needs regular maintenance, such as painting and cleaning, and it does cost more than vinyl siding.

Plywood Siding

Plywood siding is the least expensive of the wood siding because it is installed during the framing of the home and provides the structural properties and siding in one product. It needs to be sealed by either a stain or a paint making it a high-maintenance material. It also has a cheap look to it, and there is less material on the outside of the home since it acts as both the sheathing and the siding.

Fiber-cement Siding

Fiber-cement siding, also known as HardiPlank and HardiPanel, is a cementous material embedded with cellulose fibers, making it durable, strong, and resistant to moisture. Fiber-cement siding can look like wood, stucco, or masonry. It is rot- and termite-proof with a warranty up to 50 years and is noncombustible, yet it will accept paint like wood siding does. The disadvantages are that it is fairly heavy to work with, is more expensive than vinyl siding, and needs to be painted regularly.

Replacing this type of siding is similar to wood siding. You must first remove the damaged area of the board and replace it with the same type, prime it, and then paint it.

Aluminum, Steel, and Vinyl Siding

Metal siding became popular in the '60s and '70s, and vinyl siding became popular in the '70s and '80s since it is easy to install and requires low to no maintenance. Interlocking siding is the most popular type of metal or vinyl siding. Steel and aluminum siding imitates the look of wood better than vinyl and hides the wall's imperfections better than vinyl since it is more rigid. No painting is required, and this type of siding will not flake, crack, rot, or chip—and it's noncombustible. The problem with metal siding is that it can dent if hit hard enough and can show scratches. In addition, chalking can occur due to oxidation and can fade the color in time.

Vinyl siding comes in various colors, shapes, and texture and is the least expensive siding. It will not dent, flake, or rot and painting is never required. Aside from periodic cleaning, it is relatively maintenance free. The disadvantages include it chipping and cracking if hit hard, the color fading over time if exposed to extremely low temperatures, and it not hiding wall imperfections as well as metal does.

The various trim pieces work together to hold each other in place. The bottom edge of each piece of vinyl siding overlaps and clicks into the locking channel of the top of the piece below it (see Figure 9.3). When these panels lock into place, they seal out water; however, water can easily get into these channels at the end and at the joints. Manufacturers make weep holes in the bottom of siding to allow the water to escape if this happens. I recommend flashing around all doors and windows before installing siding to help direct the water away from the house in case any water does get behind the siding. Vinyl siding needs room to expand and contract, so never butt up the ends against the trim; make sure your trim pieces overlap the ends of the siding enough to keep water from entering the ends. Independent contractors usually install the siding, and the manufacturer's warranty does not cover the installation. If you hear vinyl siding making popping and cracking noises as the sun strikes it in the early morning, your siding is probably nailed too tightly. Vinyl needs to be nailed loosely enough to allow it to expand and contract with enough room on the sides next to the trim.

The upsides to vinyl and aluminum siding are that it can be installed over almost any previous exterior covering without removing the existing surface and it requires very little maintenance. The downside is that it costs two to three times the cost of an exterior paint job; therefore, it needs to last at least two to three times as long as paint. (A properly prepared exterior paint job should last about 8-10 years before it needs to be repainted.) Vinyl can crack easily in low temperatures and, when replacing either vinyl or aluminum, it can be hard to exactly match color, texture, and shape. The finish of aluminum siding can chalk, fade, or discolor from the harsh rays of the sun, rain, and airborne pollutants.

FIGURE 9.3

Vinyl and metal siding interlocks with the preceding piece.

However, a thorough cleaning may be all your vinyl or aluminum siding needs to restore it to looking like new. There are various products that will clean your siding, but you can make your own formula out of 1 gallon of hot water, 1 cup of laundry detergent, 1 cup of powdered household cleaner (such as Spic & Span or Soilax), and 3/4 cup of laundry bleach. The detergent and powdered cleaner will wash away dirt and chalking, while the bleach will remove any dark mildew stains.

Follow these steps when washing metal or vinyl siding:

1. Spray an area of siding with a hose, making sure it is wet, to remove any dirt or grime.

2. Wash the siding using an automotive pole; use a pole that's at least 6 feet long or one that extends. This will make it easier on you and your back. Dip the brush in the cleaning solution and wash from the ground up to prevent staining. You can also use a garden sprayer to apply the cleaning solution to avoid having to continually dip the brush.

> **CAUTION**
>
> Always protect your bushes, trees, and plants when cleaning your siding. You can buy environmentally safe products if you are worried about your plants.

3. Let the solution sit on the siding a few minutes while you are washing a different area, but do not allow it to dry.

4. Rinse from the top down.

5. For stubborn stains or mildew, you can use a more concentrated cleaning product or a mildew remover.

6. Use a power washer that is low power and use it at eye level, making sure you do not spray water up underneath the siding since this causes moisture to get behind the siding. If you use a heavy-duty power washer, you want to make sure you stand far enough away so the pressure of the water doesn't dent the metal or vinyl siding. There are various low-power washers for cars and homes that have a soft scrub brush attachment and combine both the cleaning solution with the water.

I have a hard time suggesting you paint your vinyl or metal siding because, by doing so, you turn your siding from a low-maintenance material to a high-maintenance issue. Once you paint the siding, you are exposing yourself to peeling paint and continual painting down the road. If you do want to paint your siding, make sure you buy a proper exterior paint that will adhere to metal or vinyl, depending on the type of siding you have.

Replacing Vinyl Siding

Whether you had a storm peel off your siding or just a damaged piece, replacing vinyl siding is easy because it is so flexible and easy to cut. First, you must buy a removal tool (costing about $5–$7) to remove the panel and tin snips to cut it to size. Hopefully, the builder left some vinyl siding panels in your basement, attic, or garage in case you needed them in the future. Sometimes it is hard to find the exact color, size, and sheen to match. I suggest visiting a local siding dealer to see if they know where you can buy a panel to match the existing siding. Obviously, if you are planning on installing siding, always leave yourself enough for future repairs.

Repairing or Replacing Aluminum Siding

Scratched or corroded areas can be touched up easily by using a metal primer first. After it has dried, touch it up with an exterior paint that matches the siding color and sheen.

Aluminum siding can be dented fairly easily. For a large dent, you can drill in a screw and pull the head of it out to unpop the dent. Then fill the hole with a two-part auto body filler. You can also fill in dents with this same two-part auto body filler. Sand the area after it has dried, prime it, and paint it.

You may have to replace an entire panel or section. This requires cutting out the damaged area and replacing it with the same siding or finding some that is similar.

Stucco

Stucco is a popular siding material used in warm climates. Traditional stucco is made of cement, sand, and lime and has been used since Renaissance days. Stucco dries hard and is moisture resistant. Asphalt-impregnated felt is a type of building paper often used to wrap a house before applying stucco. Wire lath is attached on top of the paper with spacer nails holding the wire 1/4" away. (Wire lath is not needed when applying stucco over masonry walls or concrete block.) Three coats are then added to give the stucco a thick coat without cracking (see Figure 9.4). The first coat is the scratch coat and is about 3/8" thick, similar to plaster walls. The second coat is the brown coat and is about 3/8" thick; the last, or top, coat is about 1/8" to 1/4" thick and usually has a pigment of an earth tone to give the stucco its color.

The ideal temperature for applying stucco is 50°–80° F. You can buy synthetic stucco that looks authentic for patching areas, but it doesn't hold up as well as genuine stucco. I suggest that you hire this job out to a professional.

Brick

A popular exterior covering is brick, which is made of fired clay and is available in various colors. Brick is desirable since it can last centuries and rarely needs much maintenance the first 25 years after installation. Brick veneers are also becoming popular because they are less expensive and give the look of real brick. Unfortunately, brick veneers do not last as long.

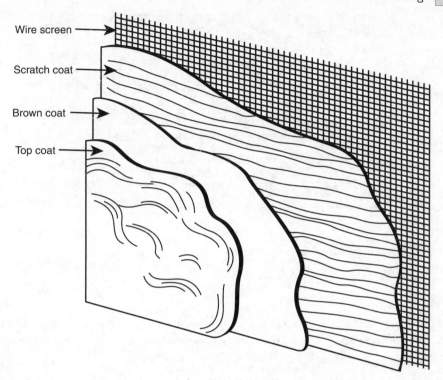

Wire screen

Scratch coat

Brown coat

Top coat

FIGURE 9.4

Three coats of stucco: scratch coat, brown coat, and top coat.

Once a year I recommend cleaning your brick. Take a garden hose and wash the dirt off the brick. You may need to do spot cleaning to remove any mold or mildew. You can buy a product to eliminate mold, or you can use 1 cup of bleach with 1 gallon of water. Use a stiff nylon brush and wear goggles to protect your eyes. Make sure you soak the brick first before cleaning off the mold so the brick doesn't absorb the bleach; then rinse thoroughly. Be sure to protect your vegetation and buy an environmentally safe product if you have plants or bushes near your home.

Brick can be susceptible to water damage by either rain hitting the brick and soaking into the mortar, causing the joints to crack, or by wicking ground water up into the brick and mortar, causing the salt crystals in the mortar to break down the mortar.

First, you want ensure proper drainage around your home by installing a foundation drain or changing the slope of your yard to cause the water to run away from your home. Then, you should repoint the mortar joints between the brick with new mortar, filling the cracks and holes (see Figure 9.5).

FIGURE 9.5

Repoint brick joints if there is cracking.

Stone

Stone is the most durable and expensive material you can choose for your exterior. Because of this expense, manufacturers have made precast stone veneers to look like stone and yet be affordable.

Like a brick wall, you will need to make sure the wall is cleaned once a year, keeping an eye out for mold and removing it when spotted. The mortar can break down from time to time and will need to be repointed.

CHECKLIST

❑ Sheathing should be covered with house wrap or building felt.

❑ Prep wood siding properly before painting it by removing chipping, sanding it, and caulking.

❑ Use a mildew-resistant additive with your house paint.

❑ Wash vinyl or metal siding from the ground up, and rinse from the top down.

❑ Remove mold from the side of your home with a mildew killer and scrub brush.

❑ Repoint the joints between brick when cracks appear.

FIREPLACES AND WOOD STOVES

This is one of my favorite tongue twisters my grandfather taught me: A flea, a fly in a flue. Imprisoned so what could they do? Said the flea let us fly, said the fly let us flee, so they flew through a flaw in the flue.

Let's face it, a fireplace spells out romance like nothing else in a home, which is why it is the focal point in a room. Owning a home with a fireplace comes with a good bit of responsibility and maintenance, though.

CARING FOR YOUR FIREPLACE OR WOOD STOVE

When you buy a home with a fireplace or wood stove, you should always have the chimney inspected to make sure it is in proper working order. The inspector will check the brick and mortar to make sure there are no cracks and no missing brick or stone. If you have a wood stove, the chimney is metal and the inspector will look to make sure all the screws are in place and there is no rusting. Again, you do not want any cracks or holes in your chimney.

Chimney Sweeps

It's a good idea to have a chimney sweep (the name of the professional) clean and inspect the chimney every year for a couple reasons. First, you want to remove the risk of fire; second, you want to maintain the efficiency of your fireplace or wood

TIP

By burning dry hardwoods, you can decrease the buildup of creosote, which is caused by burning woods that are not seasoned or are wet. Soft woods are considered to be more creosote producing than hardwoods are, but the real problem is unseasoned or wet wood no matter whether it is soft or hard. Season firewood for 6 months under a tarp or under cover. Another option is to burn fire logs that are made of sawdust and petroleum wax. These logs burn much cleaner and minimize creosote buildup.

stove. Chimney sweeps clean out the soot, when it reaches 1/8" thick, and the creosote, which is produced by an incomplete combustion of wood. Both creosote and soot are flammable, although soot is softer and easier to clean than creosote.

Chimney Caps

It is important to have a properly fitting chimney cap on the top of your chimney so birds and animals don't nest in it. The cap will also help to protect your chimney from water damage and debris that could block the hole and cause carbon monoxide to back up into your house.

There are three types of chimney caps: outside mount, inside mount for a metal flue, and inside mount for a tile flue. The outside mount fits over the flue (chimney) and should cover about 2" or 3" of the top of the flue. You will need to tighten the screws on all sides of the chimney cap to keep it firmly in place. An inside chimney cap for a metal flue needs to be pushed firmly into the flue—metal flues get too hot to use sealer. An inside cap for a round tile flue also needs to be pushed into the flue and then sealed with a silicone sealer.

Always follow the manufacturer's instructions, and check your chimney cap often to make sure it is in good shape. If you are afraid of heights or uncomfortable working on your roof, hire a professional.

If you have smoke coming into your home, check to see if the damper is open. The *damper* is the door or vent in the chimney that acts as a valve to regulate the draft. You need to open the damper to allow the air and heat to properly flow to keep the fire burning.

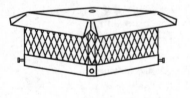

Outside mount

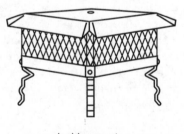

Inside mount

FIGURE 10.1

Types of chimney caps.

For maximum wood burning, buy seasoned wood that has been dried out for at least 6 months. It will burn hotter and decrease your chances of creosote buildup. In green wood, 50% of the weight is made up of moisture, making it much harder to burn and producing less heat.

WOOD STOVES

When buying a wood stove, look at the sticker to make sure it is EPA approved. It will also show you the *BTU rating*, which is the amount of heat it can produce. This is important to know to buy the right size for your room or living space. Most wood stoves put out between 15,000 and 30,000 BTU. The number of windows and doors you have will determine how big a unit you will need. A wood stove won't heat your entire house in most cases, but it can provide 50%–80% of your home's heat load. Always know the square footage of your room and home before shopping for a wood stove.

You can buy two types of wood burning stoves: catalytic combustor or noncatalytic combustor. A *catalytic combustor* achieves a slow and controlled combustion of the wood. This burns off the smoke that causes soot and creosote buildup. It needs minimal cleaning, and the face of the combustor can be cleaned with a brush. The internal honeycomb of the combustor should be replaced every 2 or 3 years during normal use. If you start to get excessive smoke coming out of the chimney, then you know you need a new combustor. A *noncatalytic combustor* has a heavy-duty insulated firebox that keeps the heat in and helps to burn the wood more efficiently by burning more gases and reducing soot and creosote.

When purchasing a wood stove, buy one that is at least 1/4" thick and made of plate steel or cast iron. Always buy the best you can afford and have it professionally installed for safety reasons. You will need to have proper clearance in order for the wood stove to work properly and safely.

PROPER FIREPLACE AND WOOD STOVE SAFETY

Follow these tips to operate your fireplace or wood stove safely (see Figure 10.2):

- Make a fire by opening the glass doors or screen curtains of your fireplace and set the kindling/newspaper underneath the logs. The logs should be placed on top of

> **TIP**
>
> Before you start the first fire of the season, be sure you check the top of your chimney with a flashlight to make sure there are no birds or animals living in it. If there are, chances are good that there is a young one living with mama and papa. Wait until the baby is old enough to be on its own; then call your county's wildlife removal team and they will safely remove the animals. After that experience, you will run to the home center to buy a chimney cap!

> **TIP**
>
> Light a match and then blow it out. If the smoke goes up the chimney, then the damper is open.

the fireplace crate. Open the damper and a window in your home a couple of inches to create a draft. Now light the kindling. After the fire has caught, you can close the window—provided there is enough draft to keep the fire lit. This is true for a wood stove, too, unless you have a pellet wood stove.

- Keep the glass doors or metal curtains closed to keep sparks from entering the room.

- Keep a fire extinguisher close by the fireplace or wood stove.

- Purchase a nonflammable rug to put directly in front of the fireplace or wood stove to protect your carpet or floor. These can be found at fireplace stores.

- Always keep a close eye on a fire when children are present, and never let them play with the fire.

- When removing coals, make sure they are completely out. Wait 3 days after a fire before scooping them into a bag and throwing them away. Open the damper when pulling out the ash so the loose ash will float up the chimney and not in your face. Leave a layer of ash to help insulate the coals in your next fire. (Don't be a dumb ash. Never vacuum ashes in case there is a hot coal hiding in the ash.)

- Hire a chimney sweep once a year.

Use a creosote cleaner to remove the black creosote from the outside brick hearth. Clean the glass doors by scraping off any residue from the fire with a razor blade after the glass has cooled. Then clean with a glass cleaner. You can purchase all these products at a fireplace store or possibly at a hardware store.

CHECKLIST

❑ Have your chimney inspected every year, and have a chimney sweep clean your fireplace every couple of years, as needed.

❑ If buying a wood burning stove, buy one recommended by the EPA.

❑ Install a chimney cap to keep your chimney protected from rain and animals from nesting in the flue.

❑ Burn hardwoods to cut down creosote and soot buildup.

❑ Open the flue and crack open a window to create a draft up the chimney. This will help your fire to burn efficiently.

❑ Always remove ash from your fireplace safely.

11

FLOORING

A common question asked on *Talk2DIY* on The DIY Network is, "Can I refinish my hardwood floors?" The answer is yes, but don't try it. Granted, it's tempting when you walk by those rental drum sanders in hardware stores and think you can save yourself a good bit of money doing the work yourself, but my experience has been that most people mess up their beautiful hardwood floors because they are novices. Refinishing your hardwood floors takes skill and know-how. Operating a drum sander is a skill in itself and not something you should learn while practicing on your own floor.

Hardwood floors are just one type of floor covering available. Other materials such as ceramic or clay tile, vinyl tile, sheet vinyl, linoleum, cork, bamboo, and carpet or rugs are also great options depending on the area of your home's floor you plan on covering. Before I get into the types of coverings, let's take a look at the subfloor.

IN THIS CHAPTER

- Installing the proper subfloor

- Choosing the right flooring material for your room

- Properly cleaning and caring for your floors

SUBFLOOR

Underneath every floor covering lays a subfloor. The thickness and type of subfloor you should have depends on the floor covering you will be using. For instance, a hardwood floor requires a 3/4" plywood or oriented strand board (OSB) subfloor. I prefer plywood over OSB for subfloors because floors are susceptible to water spills and water breaks down OSB more than it does plywood. Also, tiling is never recommended directly over OSB. A tile floor requires a 3/4" thick plywood subfloor with a 1/2" cement backer board leveled to keep the floor rigid. Unlike tile, carpet and sheet vinyl are flexible and do not require the subfloor to be perfectly level. Laminate floor systems are *floating floors*, meaning they are not attached to the subfloor below and therefore can be laid on concrete or a wood subfloor.

The subfloor is screwed or nailed to the joists below it. The *joists* are the horizontal flooring supports that are either 24" or 16" apart. It is recommended you have the joists 16" apart O.C. (on center) if you are tiling a floor because of the weight of the tile, glue, and grout.

If you are planning on installing radiant heat, you will need to install the system in the concrete slab before you lay your subfloor for hydronic (water) radiant heat or on top of your subfloor if you are using electric radiant heat.

TIP

I'm a firm believer in using screws instead of nails to lay the subfloor. Screws are less likely to pull up and you are therefore less likely to have a squeaky floor due to the subfloor.

FLOORING MATERIALS

The various types of flooring materials include sheet vinyl, vinyl tiles, linoleum, hardwood floors, laminate or engineered floors, ceramic or clay tile, stone tile, and carpet.

Sheet vinyl, vinyl tile, and linoleum are generally used in the kitchen, the bath, entryways, laundry rooms, rec rooms, and any area that may receive spills. These are popular floor coverings because they're relatively inexpensive and offer endless patterns and colors from which to choose. The tiles are easy to install, but the seams can collect dirt and liquids can potentially seep through the seams to the subfloor.

Vinyl or linoleum is easy to clean and maintain by vacuuming, sweeping, or mopping it regularly. You can quickly clean spots and spills with a mild detergent and water. A weekly cleaning with a commercial floor cleaner for vinyl is recommended.

Hardwood floors last longer than any other flooring (a lifetime) and can add value to your home. They can be refinished several times, and more often if you have solid 3/4" hardwood floors. There are many types of wood to choose from, with oak, pine, and maple being the most popular. Bamboo flooring hit the market a few years ago and has proven to be a beautiful flooring material. Cork floors are also beautiful and extremely durable while looking exotic and offering a decent amount of acoustical soundproofing below. Hardwood floors require a professional to sand the finish and stain them. Unfinished flooring allows you to color the floor with any stain color you choose. You must finish this flooring with a glossy or matte finish, however. You can use oil-based or water-based finishes, but I suggest using an oil-based polyurethane finish and applying two or three coats to the stained hardwood. You can use a glossy or matte finish, but remember that a glossy finish will reflect sunlight, making it bright in sunny rooms and sometimes hard on the eyes because of the glare. Prefinished flooring comes in hardwood boards that have been finished at the factory and are installed prefinished. Hardwood floors are perfect for the majority of the interior areas of your home.

Laminate or engineered flooring consists of two or more layers or wood. The top layer is usually a laminate or hardwood veneer, while the lower layers are softwood. Floating floors are not nailed or glued to the subfloor; the boards are often glued to each other.

You should clean wood flooring with a vacuum to remove dust and dirt once a week and wipe it down with a dust mop at least as often. Water is an enemy to wood floors so remove any water immediately.

Clay-based ceramic tiles are great to have in your kitchen, bathroom, mudrooms, entry-ways, and anywhere you want a durable and low-maintenance floor. Ceramic tiles come in four types: glazed tile, patio tile, quarry tile, and paver tile. The body of the tile is made for the specific need of the tile. The thickness, the composition of the tile, and the temperature and duration of the firing or baking of the tile determine the strength of the tile. A tile dealer will help you pick out the proper tile for your needs. Tiles can get rather expensive depending on what look you want. Always follow the manufacturer's instructions on curing time, sealing the tile, and proper grout and cleaning products. Clay-based ceramic tile can last a lifetime, although you may have to replace a broken tile from time to time.

Clean your tiles regularly and remove dirt with a broom or vacuum weekly. Hot water and a mild detergent should wipe away most stains. You might want to check with your tile dealer to see whether there is a recommended cleaner for your particular tiles.

Stone tiles are made of real stone that has been sliced from boulders into a variety of shapes and sizes. Stone tiles such as marble need to be properly installed and should be handled by a professional. Stone tile can last a lifetime. Check the manufacturer's directions for the proper cleaning products.

> **TIP**
>
> If you have ceramic or stone tile installed in your home, always ask for some extra tile in case you need to replace a broken tile in the future and want to match the color and pattern.

Carpet offers warmth and softness under your feet. Area rugs, on the other hand, are nice for a splash of color and coziness without installing wall-to-wall carpet. Carpet is made of a face pile and a backing that holds it together. The face pile comes in cut and loop variations. The cut pile stands straight up, whereas the loop construction consists of the yarn that loops over and returns into the backing. Some carpets mix cut and loop together to form a texture. Multitextures hold up to footprints and soil well, and the heavier the carpet, the longer and better it will hold up. Select a carpet for its density, pile height, and fiber content. I've laid my own carpet and would never do it again. This is heavy work and requires a very strong person with good knees to kick-in the carpet to the tack boards. Tack boards are nailed around the perimeter of the room in two rows with the tacks facing the wall. When the carpet is kicked and stretched in place, the tacks grab onto the backing and hold the carpet in place.

| Chapter 11 | Flooring |

If you have allergies, carpet and area rugs are not for you. Get one of the other flooring options that can easily be swept clean. Carpets should be vacuumed regularly to remove dust and dirt. Many products on the market can remove stains as well as pet odors from your carpet. Many grocery stores rent cleaning machines that will make your carpet look like new.

CHECKLIST

❑ Choose the proper thickness of subfloor for your flooring material.

❑ Always hire a professional to install and refinish your hardwood floors.

❑ Hire a professional to install your carpet.

❑ Never use carpet if you have bad allergies.

FOUNDATION

As I stated in Chapter 3, "Basements," I grew up in a home
with a basement. Our foundation consisted of a 4" slab concrete floor and cinder block walls. Before the basement was
finished, the concrete slab made a perfect roller rink, and the
cinder block walls had one opening for a crawl space underneath the front porch. It made the perfect theatre for my
brother's seventh birthday party. Our parents pulled a sheet
over half the opening and we tossed a plastic hook that was
fastened to a fishing pole line over the sheet. As soon as my
dad could put a plastic toy on the hook, he (the fish) would
give three strong tugs to pull the prize out of the hole. While
the giant fish gave toys to these fascinated kids, I was con-
sumed with worry about my father being in the eerie crawl
space amongst spiders and possibly finding our hidden comic
books.

Eventually, the hole was blocked up and the basement was finished. Had I never seen the basement raw, I would have never
appreciated what our house was sitting on.

FOUNDATION TYPES

The foundation is one of the most important components of
your home. The type of foundation is dictated by your area's
local building codes. These codes take into account the type of
soil, the frostline, the landscape of the lot, and the depth of
the water table.

There are four main types of foundations: slab, crawlspace,
basement, pole, and pier or post.

Slab

The slab foundation is usually 4"–6" thick concrete, and the frame of the house sits on the slab. Before the concrete is poured, gravel is laid out and leveled to help drainage below the slab. There is a trench dug along the perimeter of the slab down to the frostline; this is known as the *footing* (see Figure 12.1). Many times the pipes for plumbing and the utility hookups run in the slab. When the concrete is poured, the pipes are then buried in the concrete. Rebar, too, is used in some slab foundations to give added support. Expansion joints are sometimes needed if there is a chance of cracking when the concrete is curing.

The slab foundation is used in areas where there is high clay content or in sandy areas such as Florida. This is the least expensive and the fastest foundation to build since it needs little excavation and is poured at the same time with the footings. The slab foundation and footings should last up to 200 years.

Crawlspace

A *crawlspace* foundation is where the home's main floor is approximately 2' off the ground level (see Figure 12.2). Similar to a slab foundation, the footings are extended to the frost line. The walls are extended from the footings around the perimeter of the home's layout. This type of foundation makes it very easy to run the pipes and wires for plumbing and electricity. The crawlspace foundation is fairly inexpensive since it doesn't require much excavation or concrete, with the exception of the footings and stem walls.

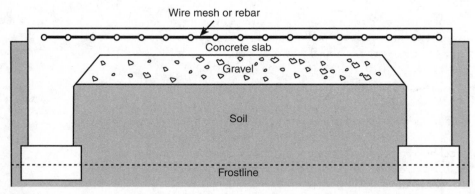

FIGURE 12.1

Slab foundation with footing down to the frostline.

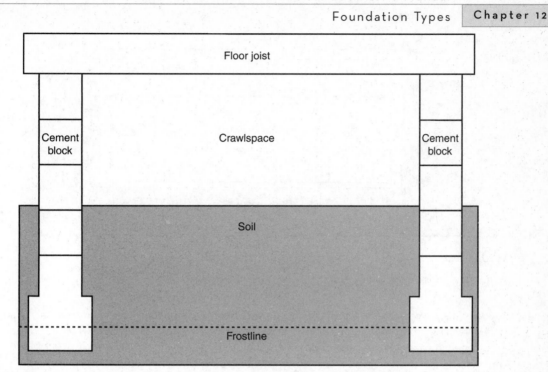

FIGURE 12.2

A crawlspace foundation above the ground level.

Standard Basement Foundation and Other Types of Basements

A *basement* foundation is nice because it offers more space to a home. In most cases, the basement foundation is the same square footage as the living space above and can serve as a storage space or as a finished living area. Figure 12.3 shows a standard basement. Basements are not used in areas with unsettled soil or a high water table because of potential cracking in the foundation walls due to flooding or hydrostatic pressure.

The basement foundation is a combo of slab and crawlspace. The slab is poured and then the walls are either poured concrete or concrete block walls with rebar, depending on your local codes. Concrete block will last 100 years or more.

This is the most expensive type of foundation since it requires more labor to excavate the land, dig 8' below the frostline, pour a concrete slab, and then pour the concrete walls or lay the concrete blocks. Pouring the concrete can take up to three days and then take a week to set before you can start building on top of it.

Chapter 12   Foundation

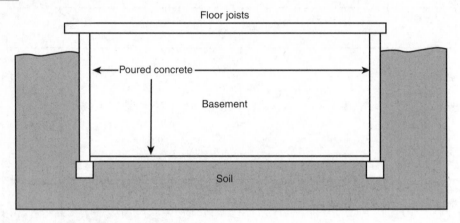

FIGURE 12.3

A standard basement foundation.

This type of basement foundation can be dark. It is important to remember that, when finishing a basement, you need to install a window well and a window wide and deep enough to escape in case of an emergency.

Daylight Basement

This is the type of basement I grew up with. This basement foundation is the same as the previous one, except it is built on a sloping lot: front to back or left to right. This basement opens to an outdoor space, usually to a backyard (see Figure 12.4). The advantage to this type of basement is the extra light and the indoor/outdoor space. Usually there are sliding glass or French doors that lead to the outside.

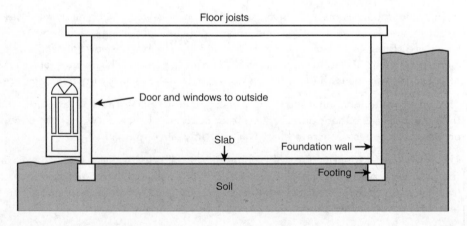

FIGURE 12.4

A daylight basement that opens onto an outdoor space.

Partial Basement

Most basements are the same square footage as the living area above them. In areas with unstable soil or rocky conditions, however, you can put in a partial basement, which is usually less than 75% of the main floor plan (see Figure 12.5). Some homes have partial daylight basements (see Figure 12.6). The slope of the land allows a basement under part of the main floor, and the basement opens onto an outside space.

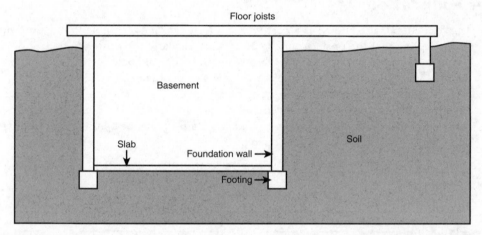

FIGURE 12.5

A partial basement.

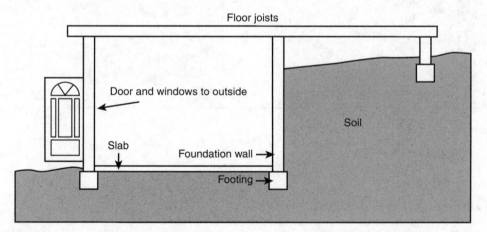

FIGURE 12.6

A partial daylight basement.

Pole Foundation

When a home is built over water or in flood plains, this is the foundation of choice. The metal poles, or wood posts, allow the main floor to be built well above ground. These posts allow water to rise underneath the house without causing any damage. The posts are tied into beams that form a stem wall around the perimeter of the home.

Pier Foundation

This foundation, also known as a *post foundation*, is similar to the pole foundation with the exception that the posts are made of cement. Similarly, the posts are tied into beams to form the stem wall along the perimeter. You would only use this type of foundation if you lived in conditions such as coastal or mountainous areas in which you would need to drill into rock, place steel rods, and pour in the concrete. Cement posts have the advantage over wood post/pole foundations because the posts are insect resistant and more durable. The pier foundation can sometimes be used with wooden posts. Figure 12.7 shows a pier foundation.

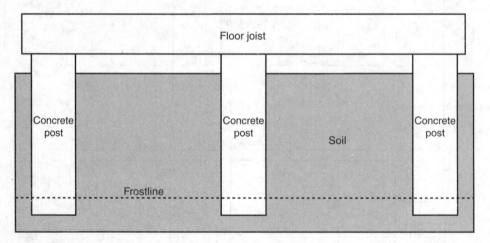

FIGURE 12.7

A pier foundation.

FOUNDATION PROBLEMS

Many serious foundation problems are the result of trees being too close to the house or the type of soil around the foundation. Clay soil has a hard time absorbing water and can cause problems. Too much water can cause clay soil to heave and disrupt the foundation's integrity. Large trees use an enormous amount of water and can quickly draw out the moisture in the ground. The roots can push against the foundation, though, causing it to crack through time.

The worst type of soil for a foundation contains expandable clay or peat. The best type of soil is *virgin* soil, which is soil that has never been disturbed. Hire a soil engineer to evaluate your soil conditions; he can tell you what you need to do to bring the foundation up to code.

Water can be a disaster to your home's foundation and interior. Too much or too little water can cause structural problems to the foundation. Too much water can cause hydrostatic pressure against the foundation walls or footing. *Hydrostatic pressure* is the pressure water creates when it builds up against a surface such as your foundation wall. The pressure is so great it starts to crack and buckle the wall itself and pushes water through the cracks. Usually water gets through the joint where the slab and wall meet. Concrete is made of lime cement and stone. A chalky appearance on the inside of the walls happens when water pushes through the wall and pushes out the lime that holds it together. Over time, this leads to a chemical breakdown in the bonding of the wall.

Too little water is also a concern. The moisture in the soil around your foundation should remain as constant as possible. Ideally, the soil should be damp 4'-5' deep. In areas of the country that have dry seasons, you might want to use a watering system for your plants and trees or soaker hoses to keep the soil moist.

Since water can be such a problem to the integrity of your foundation and can ruin your belongings inside, you might want to waterproof the outside of your foundation walls. Most likely, the contractor will dig a trench around the walls and footings and coat the outside walls with a waterproofing material. This can be costly but well worth it.

The following are some tell-tale signs of foundation problems:

- Cracks in the slab foundation
- Windows and doors getting stuck
- Nail pops in the walls and ceilings
- Plaster walls cracking
- Floors cracking

NOTE

My friend, Cissy, was selling another friend, Vikki's, home last year. Two days before they were closing on the home, Cissy got a phone call from the buyer stating that the insurance company wouldn't insure the home with the tree in the front yard so close to the house. They said it would compromise the foundation. Vikki had to cut the tree down and remove the roots before she could close on the house and sign the papers with the buyers.

CAUTION

Overwatering your gardens can be harmful, too. This causes hydrostatic pressure against the foundation of your home.

- Chimneys cracking or leaning
- Doors and windows having visible gaps that were not there before

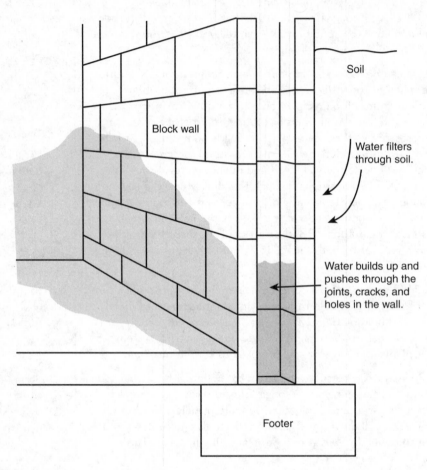

FIGURE 12.8

Hydrostatic pressure can push water into the basement's walls.

If you have any of these problems, there is a good chance that your foundation is being compromised. Always call in a structural engineer or a contractor who is a foundation specialist to give you the right advice and ensure your safety when a crack is over 1/4" in width.

The following are possible solutions for any foundation problems you might have:

- You can use various pier systems to pin the foundation and stabilize a cracked or bowing basement wall.

- Reinforce the foundation walls by pumping in cement through small holes in the slab (known as *slabjacking*) or placing mechanical jacks that lift up settled beams. *Crack injection* is also popular. This injected polymer fills the full depth of the crack to prevent further deterioration. Always hire a concrete repair specialist for problems with your foundation walls.

- Soil densification is an efficient way to compact loose soil around your foundation. Loose soil could be caused by a lack of moisture and/or a foundation built on fill soil rather than virgin soil. Fill soil needs to be compacted.

- Load transfer can help transfer the load in a cracked slab by composite inserts or steel dowel bar retrofit in between the joints or cracks.

- Slab lifting is a process where holes are drilled in the concrete slab and then concrete is poured in those holes to lift the concrete up from underneath. This will level off the slab and possibly help fix a cracking foundation wall, depending on your situation.

Even if you find that a crack is not compromising the foundation, fix it immediately. You want to make sure it looks cosmetically pleasing, but more importantly, you want to prevent further damage. Use a vinyl repair patch or a latex concrete caulk to fill in gaps.

The following are some things you can do to avoid foundation problems in the first place:

- Make sure the slope of your lawn is graded away from the walls of your home, or you may need to install a foundation drain. If you are unable to regrade your lawn or your neighbor's lawn slopes down to yours, you will need to install a foundation drain or possibly a French drain further away from your home. Hire a professional to assess your problem.

- Water your plants and grass evenly around the home and do not overwater.

- Do not plant trees or garden beds with heavy root systems close to the house.

- Always fix leaky plumbing or sewage pipes immediately.

- Rout the downspout of your gutter system away from the home.

Chapter 12 | Foundation

CHECKLIST

❑ Keep an eye out for cracks in your foundation walls, slab, and plaster walls and windows and doors not shutting properly. Call a professional to look at the situation if you notice cracks in your foundation or your window or doors are not shutting properly.

❑ Fix any cracks immediately to head off further problems.

❑ Divert water away from the home.

❑ Remove trees too close to your home and never plant shrubs or trees next to your home.

13

GARAGE AND OUTBUILDINGS

Recently, I went online and ordered a tool shed. Not a big tool shed, just one that would hold my ever-increasing collection of tools, boogie boards, skates...well, you get the idea...my *stuff*!

I was shocked by the delivery of my newly purchased 5'×10'×5'6" tool shed. It came in a 6' box, 14" wide and 6" deep. Need I say that when I opened the box, there was a bazillion pieces to be put together? But, I did it. You know why? Because I needed more room and it was worth the headache of putting it together to get it.

Garages and outbuildings are great spaces to put our cars and our "stuff" in and should be looked at as mini homes. Much that applies to a house applies to a garage. It needs a foundation, roof, walls, and so on. Usually, the biggest difference is how the inside is finished or not finished and the use of garage doors rather than conventional doors.

Most garages are attached to the house, and the items we put in our garages—cars, lawn mowers, solvents, and paints—can create air pollution in our homes. It is important to start your car with the garage door open. Cars give off carbon monoxide, which is a lethal gas that not only can affect the garage, but can also seep into the house. It is important to make sure all the holes between the house and the garage are sealed properly with caulk or a vinyl repair patch to keep these fumes and gases outside your home.

IN THIS CHAPTER

- Storing combustible materials safely
- Proper disposal of hazardous materials
- Removal of oil stains
- Troubleshooting garage doors

STORING FLAMMABLE MATERIALS SAFELY

The garage is a great area to store lawn mowers, paints, and solvents. However, it is important to know how to store oily or stain-soaked rags so they don't spontaneously combust. Many house fires have begun with some oily rags tossed in a heaping pile. Spontaneous ignition begins when a combustible material like a rag is heated to ignition temperature through a slow oxidation process. This oxidation process can raise the inside temperature of a pile of rags and start a fire. The same oily rag that can catch fire in a pile will not catch fire if it is laid out flat to dry individually on a flat surface.

All oil-, gas-, or paint-soaked rags should be sealed tightly in a container and then stored in a cool, well-ventilated area away from other combustibles. The other option is to lay the rags on a flat surface until they dry out completely before reusing them.

Store gasoline and other flammable fluids outdoors, and follow the manufacturer's directions on how to store and use all chemicals. Chemicals need to be stored outside in a dry place away from a heat source.

DISPOSING OF COMBUSTIBLE MATERIALS

Make sure you dispose of any unneeded old paint, motor oils, stains, solvents, gasoline, or garden chemicals properly. Your community may hold a household hazardous waste collection day where you can throw them out responsibly. Never burn hazardous products and materials or put them in the trash or down the drain. If you are unsure of your area's hazardous waste removal, call the fire department for information or look in the front of the phone book.

REMOVING OIL STAINS FROM GARAGE FLOORS

I have heard of many remedies and tried only a few. There is a product on the market that claims to remove oil stains completely, although I have never used it. In my experience, removing oil stains can be pretty hard, but you can remove most of a stain with a bit of elbow grease and scrubbing.

To remove the surface oil, sprinkle cat litter on it to soak up the oil and then dispose of it properly. Oil stains are a bit more stubborn, so make a paste of hot water and dry dish or laundry detergent. Use a stiff bristle scrub brush to scrub the area with the paste. Hose the area and let it dry.

Another method is to use a product such as Spray 'n Wash on the stain for 10 minutes along with a dry detergent. Your last option is to spray on some oven cleaner. Use this sparingly, wash it down thoroughly, and keep children and pets away from it.

Painting Garage Floors

Most likely your garage floor is made of a 4" concrete slab. There are many products that you can use to seal, stain, or paint your cement floor. Put water on the surface of the floor to see if it beads up or soaks in. If it soaks in, you will need to seal the concrete first. If the water beads up, then it is already sealed. There are various paints you can use on slab concrete; some even have a non-slip ingredient added.

Garage Doors

When shopping for garage doors, you will notice there is a wide range to choose from. Aside from the selection of styles that will go with your home, you will want to look at the thickness of the door, whether it is rust resistant, the R-Value for insulation, and the warranty on the hardware and springs. You will want to buy the best door your money will buy. The average lifespan of a garage door is between 20 and 50 years, and a garage door opener's is about 10 years.

The R-Value you will need is determined by your location. The colder the climate, the higher the R-Value. Of course, if you live in a Arizona and you want to have an air-conditioned garage or outbuilding, then you should look into a higher R-Value as well, so your utility money isn't going out the door.

It is important to have your garage doors working properly. Most people have an electric garage door that locks and adds safety to a home or an outbuilding. A broken garage door is an invitation to a robber.

Troubleshooting Your Garage Doors

The following list will help you if you experience problems with the operation of your garage door:

- If the garage door won't respond to your remote, check to see if it needs new batteries. If batteries are not the problem, then check the keypad to make sure it is working. You may need to reprogram the keypad.

- If the swing-up door sags, it is usually because the lifting mechanism can't support the weight of the door. Replace with heavy-duty garage door hardware rather than repairing it.

- If the door sticks when opening and closing, it is probably because the rollers and hinges need to be lubricated (see Figure 13.1). Check the tracks, too. Over time, debris can build up in the tracks, causing the rollers to go over speed bumps in the tracks.

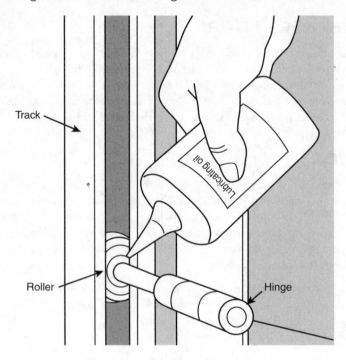

Track

Roller

Hinge

FIGURE 13.1

Lubricate the rollers.

If the doors are malfunctioning, the cable may need to be tightened without stretching the springs.

- If there isn't enough tension on the door, the springs can be tightened by unhooking them and fitting them into the next adjustment hole in the frame (see Figure 13.2). If that doesn't work, you may need new springs. Working with springs can be really dangerous; my suggestion is that you hire a professional. If you feel you can tackle this, always make sure you protect your eyes, head, and the rest of your body.

- If your spring breaks in half, you might hear a loud thud against the door. You will need to replace the spring with a similarly sized one.

- If the bar lock won't lock, the bar guide likely needs to be realigned.

- If the door rubs against the trim, you may need to adjust the brackets in the opposite direction to give the door room to move (see Figure 13.3).

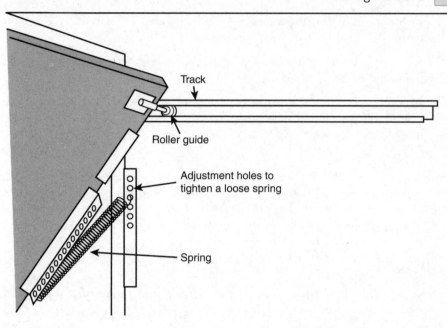

FIGURE 13.2

Tighten the loose spring by hooking it into the next hole in the track or door frame.

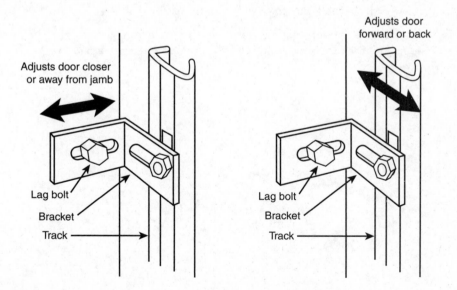

FIGURE 13.3

Adjust the brackets if the door binds or rubs against the trim.

- If the door binds, then the tracks may not be parallel. You should have room for adjustment within the hardware.

- If the door falls once it has been released, most likely the extension springs are worn out and should be replaced.

- If the door opens on its own, the extension springs are too tight and need to be replaced with looser and lighter ones.

Manual Doors

Before there were electric garage door openers, there was the manual kind. Basically, they work the same way, but they need the muscle of an arm to pull them up or down. A padlock is the way you lock these doors. The problems with these doors are much the same as garage doors with an electric opener.

CHECKLIST

❑ Plug up any holes between the garage and the house, if the garage is attached, to keep carbon monoxide outside the home.

❑ Store oily rags in a sealed container or laying flat away from combustibles until dry.

❑ Dispose of oily rags properly through your town's hazardous waste materials location.

❑ Remove oil from the floors to keep it a safe environment.

❑ Keep your garage doors in good working order by keeping the wheels lubricated, keeping the track clean, and replacing the springs when necessary.

14

HEATING AND COOLING

Before air conditioning, fans cooled off a home. The home I grew up in had an attic fan. We would open the windows and the fan would draw the air through the house and create an incredible breeze. I miss this type of home cooling system. There was something so lovely about having a constant breeze on my skin.

In the '90s I spent my summers at my friend Don's upstate New York farm that had no air conditioning. He had an entire system to keep the house cool in the summer. At night when it cooled down, all the windows were opened to let in the cooler air, so by morning the house was nice and cool. Early in the morning we would shut all the windows to lock in the cool air and pull down the shades to the windows facing the east side of the house. In the evening we would pull down the shades on the west side of the house to keep the heat out. This is how people used to live all those years without air conditioning.

When our family switched over to air conditioning, we had central air and heat installed. At the time, I felt like a Rockefeller living in the lap of luxury. Nowadays, this is common and expected.

COOLING SYSTEMS FOR YOUR HOME

There are various ways that you can keep your home cool. One way is what I described previously by locking in the cool air; another is by installing shades on your windows, which work much better than curtains. Getting glass that is Low-E is important since the film on the glass helps to keep the warm and cold temperatures outside of the home in summer and winter, respectively. Awnings are also effective to keep the sun from beating down on your home. Lastly, various trees and shrubs can offer a good bit of shade to your home. Deciduous trees are the best because they provide ample shade in the summer and lose their leaves in the winter, allowing for the heat of the sun to enter the home. Plant these trees on the east and west sides of your home and not too close to the foundation. Remember that the taller the tree, the more shade coverage you will have over your roof.

→ For more information on how Low-E glass can keep your house cooler in summer and warmer in winder, **see** "Low-E Glass," **p. 41**.

Attic fans, ceiling fans, window fans, and self-standing fans are all good to keep the air circulating and flowing. Of course, the coolest way is through air conditioning.

Fans

Installing fans in your home can help circulate the air and cool you down. Your body cools down through convection, radiation, and perspiration. *Convection* is the process of carrying heat away from your body through moving air. Air that is cooler than the skin will absorb the heat and rise. The faster the air moves, the cooler you will feel. *Radiation* is the process of transferring or radiating heat between you and objects in the home. If the objects are warmer than you, the heat will travel to you. Ventilating a room helps to remove this radiation. *Perspiration* is also a cooling mechanism. When moisture leaves the skin, it carries heat with it and removes it from the body. If there is a breeze, it will cool the skin faster by evaporating the moisture.

Attic fans are my favorite. These are installed in the ceiling and draw air from all the open windows and doors. This is good for attic ventilation, too.

Ceiling fans are used in conjunction with air conditioning to help lower your utility bill. In warm weather, you will be able to raise the thermostat 4° without feeling a reduction in comfort. Larger fan blades move more air than smaller fans. There is a switch on the housing of the fan that will allow you to reverse the direction of the blades. Switch the setting when the fan is off. In the summer, have the blades pushing the air down. In the winter, have the blades drawing up the air to the ceiling so it disperses the warmer air above up, out, and around to the floor (see Figure 14.1).

Window fans are best when used on the side of the home that has a prevailing wind. Which way the wind blows will determine if you want the fan to blow in or out. In a two-story home, use a fan to blow in air on the lower floor and have a fan blowing out on the second floor to create the best ventilation.

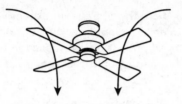

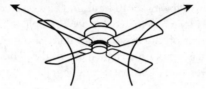

Pushing down air in summer   Pulling up air in winter

FIGURE 14.1

Adjust the switch on the fan to blow air down in the summer and pull air up in the winter.

Air Conditioning

There are a few options when it comes to air conditioning: unit air conditioners that sit in your window or an opening in your wall, a free-standing unit that is on wheels and can be rolled around in a room without a window, and central cooling systems known as central air or an HVAC (heating, venting, and air conditioning).

Unit Air Conditioners

For a small home, apartment, or studio, you will probably go for the window unit. Free-standing units are for those awkward situations where the windows aren't big enough to put in a window unit, or if you want air conditioning in the center room of a home where there isn't a window.

An air conditioner has three basic components: the condenser, the evaporator coil, and the fan or blower. The refrigerant gas is compressed and then cooled within the condenser before it goes through the evaporator coil. The blower then blows this cool air around the evaporator coil and sends the cold air into the room.

For a unit air conditioner or free-standing unit, you will want to buy the proper size for your living space. If you have a living space with an adjoining room, then you must consider the two rooms together when buying a unit. Before you go to the store, you will need to figure the square footage of the room you would like cooled. Measure the window dimensions as well, so you will know how big or small the unit will need to be to fit in the window opening.

Unit air conditioners come in three different types: window units, built-in units, and split units. Window units are installed easily into a standard double-hung window and are the least expensive. Built-in window units can also be installed in any standard double-hung window or installed into the wall, usually below a window. The built-in units have a heat pump allowing both heat and air conditioning and are therefore more expensive to buy and more expensive to run. The split system has an air compressor outside so the unit is quiet on the inside. Split units should be installed professionally. These three units usually work on a regular 110 outlet. There are heavy-duty units that require 220V of power and need to have a special outlet.

When you buy an air conditioner, you will be looking at different models and makes with various BTUs. *BTU* stands for *British thermal units*. The higher the BTUs, the more powerful the unit. Air conditioning units range from 5,000 to 18,000 BTUs. Never buy a unit too big or too small. To find out the correct BTUs for your room, find the square footage of your room (length × width = sq. ft) and multiply that number by 35 to come up with the correct BTUs. You will need to add BTUs by 10% if the room you are trying to cool is very sunny. A unit in the kitchen requires adding 4,000 more BTUs, and if there are more than two people in a room, add 600 BTUs per person.

Look for a unit with a high energy efficiency ratio (EER). The EER usually ranges from 10.0 to 16.9. The higher EER units are more expensive but cost less to run. If you plan on keeping your AC turned on all day, it's worth it to buy a unit with the highest EER you can afford. Always look for the Energy Star label as well.

When it comes to a few different models, buy the one that has at least a 1-year warranty, a temperature range of at least 20°, the temperature in 1°–2° increments, a sleep setting/energy saver button or switch, an easy-access slide-out filter, and at least three fan settings.

Central Air Conditioning

Central air is also known as HVAC since it both cools and heats the house. It is the most luxurious way to install air conditioning since it doesn't obstruct your vision out the window or take up floor space. The downside is it does require running ducts and vents throughout your entire home. For that reason, it is more expensive too, but it maintains a consistent temperature efficiently in a home, making it the best option provided you have the budget. Homes built in the last 25–30 years probably had central air conditioning installed when they were built.

An air conditioning system or HVAC consists of the following components: a compressor, a fan, a condenser coil (hot), an evaporator coil (cold), and a chemical refrigerant (see Figure 14.2). The system is split into two parts. The outside has the condensing coil, fan, and compressor. The inside components are located within the furnace. The furnace blows air through the evaporator coil that cools the air and blows it through air ducts throughout the house through the vents in each room. The temperature is adjusted through a thermostat, usually in the center of the home.

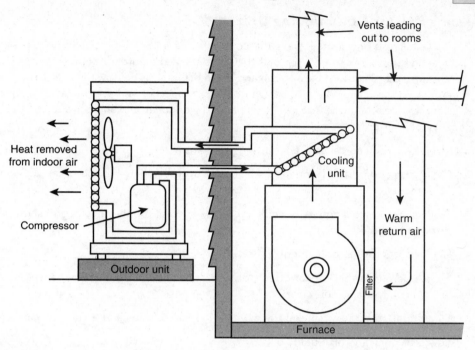

FIGURE 14.2

Components of central air conditioning.

The filter is usually located in front of the furnace and needs to be changed as often as once a month in the summer and maybe twice in the winter. The pollens and dust in the air and the amount of animals you have in your home will dictate how often you will need to change your filter. The higher the number on the filter, the more money it will cost but the more efficient it will be in not only protecting your equipment, but also cleaning the air you breathe. A dirty air filter blocks the cool air coming into your home, making the system work longer and harder.

If you are experiencing a large heat or air conditioning loss (that is, more than a few degrees), it may be more than your filter. You might need to have a technician look at your system.

Central air conditioners are rated according to their seasonal energy efficiency ratios (SEERs). This ratio is reached by taking into account the cooling output divided by the power input on the average climate in this country. The standard has been 10 since 1992 and will change to 13 in 2006. Older models will have a SEER rating of about 6 or 7.

Replacing the Air Conditioning Unit

When installing a new system, have the contractor do a Manual J calculation that will determine the proper size for the unit that consists of the outdoor compressor and condenser and the indoor blower coil and thermostat. Your new system will work better if you buy all the pieces that are designed to work together and use the latest technological advances. An undersized unit will have to work overtime and can shorten the lifespan of your unit.

An oversized unit can cause the following problems:

- Cycling on and off too frequently, which runs up your utility bill and breaks down the equipment
- Blowing excessive amounts of cold air quickly, tricking the thermostat and shutting down before the house is cooled
- Higher costs for the equipment
- Short operations that do not effectively remove the humidity and that cause problems in comfort and durability
- Large temperature swings and the inability to keep the home at a stable temperature
- Low efficiency and high utility bills
- Short equipment life
- Temperature discomfort

An undersized air conditioner has to work much harder and will eventually wear out the equipment. When you buy a unit that is the correct size, you will have improved comfort, lower utility bills, better humidity control, and fewer maintenance problems.

Buy a unit that has a thermal expansion valve (TXV) along with an EER (Energy Effeciency Ratio) greater than 11.6. Check to see if the condenser and the indoor unit meet efficiency levels that are recommended by the Consortium for Energy Efficiency (CEE). The CEE is a nonprofit, national organization that promotes energy-efficient products and services. Its website is www.cee1.org.

Always buy a unit with the Energy Star label on it. Energy Star is a government-backed program that helps businesses and consumers protect the environment through superior energy efficiency. Its website is www.energystar.gov.

Follow these guidelines for efficiency ratings:

- Central air conditioners and air-source heat pumps should have a minimum 12 SEER.
- Air-source heat pumps should have a minimum 7.6 HSPF.

- Gas-fired heat pumps should have a COP of 1.26 for heating and 1.32 for cooling.

- Thermostatic expansion valves should be greater than 11.6 EER.

Buy an air conditioner that uses a refrigerant called puron rather than freon. There have been claims that freon is destroying our ozone layers; therefore, it will be phased out by the year 2010 and could possibly be expensive when servicing your unit.

Cleaning Air Ducts

If you are experiencing a good bit of dust, vermin in the ducts, or mold you should have your ducts cleaned. Call a professional. Make sure the professional you hire is thorough and cleans all of the system's components and all the ducts and vents.

TYPES OF HEATING SYSTEMS

To heat your home, you have a few choices of furnaces or heating systems: central warm-air furnace, steam or hot water system, baseboard or radiant system, a heat pump in the case of a HVAC system, and a pipeless furnace.

Central Warm-Air Furnace

This type of furnace has a central combustor using gas, oil, or electricity to provide warm air that circulates through the house through ducts leading into all the rooms (see Figure 14.3). A forced-air furnace has a fan that forces the air through the ducts, whereas a gravity furnace circulates the air using gravity. The warm air rises through the ducts, and the cold air falls through the vents or registers returning it back to the furnace to heat it.

The most important maintenance to your system is replacing the filter. When buying replacement filters, buy a half dozen of them so you always have one on hand. If the motor runs but doesn't blow air, you might need to replace the belt. Turn off the power, remove the belt, and take it to a nearby hardware store. The bearings might need to be oiled from time to time; check your owner's manual first to find the bearings.

Steam or Hot Water System

There are two types of steam or hot water systems. The most common type supplies either steam or hot water to baseboard radiators, convectors, or heating coils in an HVAC system. The other type is a radiant system that is installed in the slab before it is poured. Radiant heat pushes the heat from the floor up, keeping your feet nice and toasty.

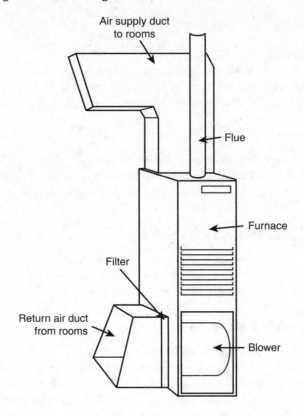

Air supply duct
to rooms

Flue

Furnace

Filter

Return air duct
from rooms

Blower

FIGURE 14.3

A central warm-air furnace forces air through ducts and vents into each room.

Baseboard and Radiant Systems

Baseboard heating units are installed low at the baseboard. The water is heated in a boiler tank that separates the water that goes to your heating system and your plumbing. Some of these heating systems have relief valves on the radiators in case the hot water gets too hot. The boilers must have pressure relief valves that release the steam buildup if it gets too hot.

If air gets trapped in a baseboard system, you can relieve the air by pressing a valve similar to a tire valve. These units need to be watched to make sure there are no leaks, and they require the fins of the units to be cleaned by a vacuum cleaner to remove the dust.

The other type of hot water system is radiant heat that carries the hot water through pipes laid in the concrete slab floor. Figure 14.4 shows a baseboard heating system.

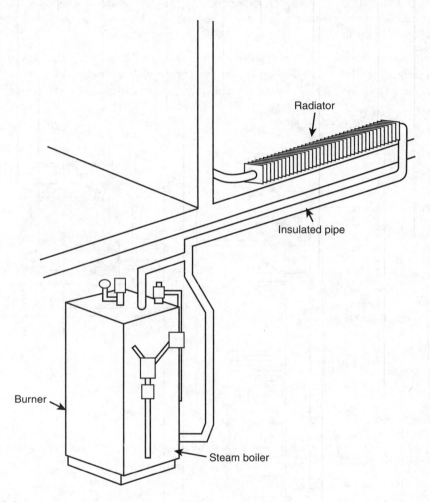

Radiator

Insulated pipe

Burner

Steam boiler

FIGURE 14.4

Baseboard heating units are installed low at the baseboard.

Heat Pump

A year-round heating and air conditioning system in which the unit supplies both hot and cool air through ducts, a heat pump consists of a compressor, coils, and a thermo-stat (see Figure 14.5).

You need to change the filter regularly (monthly when the system is operating) and have a yearly inspection by a qualified technician. If your system has an air screen or electronic air filter, be sure to clean it according to the manufacturer's instructions.

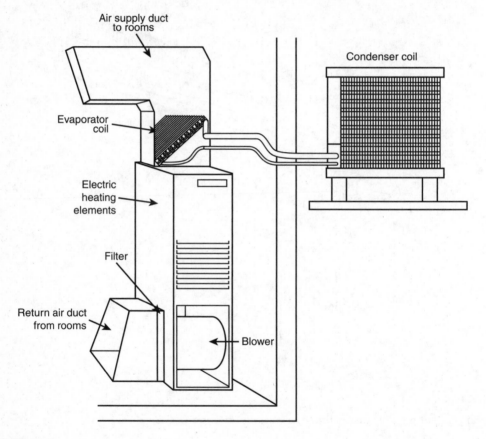

FIGURE 14.5

A heat pump in an HVAC unit.

Floor, Wall, or Pipeless Furnace

This is a ductless combustor with an enclosed chamber where fuel is burned and electrical resistance heat is generated to warm the rooms. A floor furnace is installed below the floor and provides heat for the room above (see Figure 14.6). A wall furnace is installed in a partition or an outside wall and sends heat to the rooms on each side, or one side if it is on an outside wall. A pipeless furnace is placed in the basement and sends heated air through a large register in the floor of the hallway or room above.

There is little to no maintenance on these types of furnaces. You want to make sure there is no debris around them and keep the air intake clear.

Eventually you will want to replace this system with a more modern and efficient heating system.

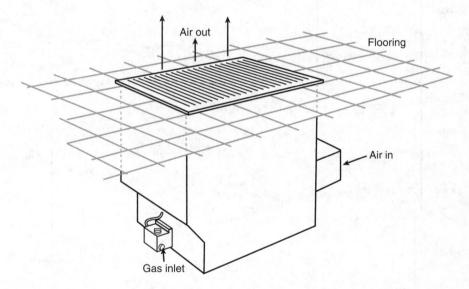

FIGURE 14.6

Floor furnaces are installed below the floor with the heated air moving up through registers in the floor.

FUEL SOURCES FOR HEATING YOUR HOME

Homes throughout the country rely on different heating and cooling systems depending on fuel source and efficiency. The various fuel sources are oil, natural gas, electricity, and wood in the case of a fireplace or wood stove.

Energy is measured in joules (J), is rated over a period of time, and is measured in watts (W). One watt being used is equivalent to 1 joule per second. Gas heaters are rated by how much energy goes into them each hour in mega joules (MJ) with 1 MJ = 1,000,000 joules. Most homes use more than 4,000 MJ every two months. Electric heaters are rated in kilowatts (kW) with 1 kW = 1,000 watts.

Electricity

Pros:

- It's available most everywhere.

- It doesn't produce pollutants in your home or the air.

- There's no need to store electricity because the power company does that for you.

- It minimizes cost by using solar, wind, or hydro.

Cons:

- Portable heaters are fairly expensive and have a small heating capacity in a large room.

- There's no heat if the power goes out.

- It's the largest producer of carbon dioxide.

Natural Gas

Pros:

- It's less expensive than electricity, although this could change by the time this book hits the shelves.

- Gas heaters have a greater capacity to heat a larger room more efficiently.

- It's the cleanest form, with less carbon dioxide than electricity.

Cons:

- It's not available everywhere.

- You need to install a flue to let the combustion gases out of the home.

- It's a nonrenewable resource.

Oil

Pros:

- Its air emissions are similar to natural gas.

- Its storage is easy and usually underground.

Cons:

- Its found only in the Northeast and Mid-Atlantic states.

- Environmental concerns exist because of leaks and soil contamination.

- Tanks sometimes have a low lifespan of 10–15 years.

- It can be more expensive, with a spike in your utility bill occuring when more oil is used October through March. The recent rise in oil prices can also be a factor.

- It's a nonrenewable resource.

Solid Fuels (Firewood and Coal)

Pros:

- Both are available everywhere.

- They have the lowest output of carbon dioxide.

Cons:

- You need to store the wood or coal.

- Requires a constant loading of the wood or coal.

- Cleanup of the mess is required.

- You need a chimney.

- They both contribute to air pollution.

- Firewood can be fairly expensive.

TIPS FOR LOWERING YOUR UTILITY BILL

Follow these tips to keep your utility bill low:

- Shade a window air conditioner from the sun to reduce its workload.

- Call a professional to tune up your heat pump, furnace, boiler, or air conditioner. Check and clean your air conditioner every year.

- Vacuum air vents, heaters, and radiators to remove dust.

| Chapter 14 | Heating and Cooling |

- Close vents and shut the doors to rooms that are not used.

- Seal and insulate your ducts.

- Insulate your home properly with the correct R-Value insulation for your area. Check your attic, garage walls, basement, and crawlspace.

→ For more information about R-Value insulation, **see** "R-Value," **p. 116**.

- Caulk all cracks in walls and around windows, doors, and trim.

- Open foundation vents in the spring and close them in the fall.

→ For more information about foundations vents, **see** "Foundation Vents," **p. 121**.

- Keep shrubs away from the back of your air conditioner unit so the air can flow properly.

- Use ceiling fans to promote air circulation, cooling in the summer and distributing heat in the winter.

CHECKLIST

❑ Select the right fan(s) to cool your home without air conditioning.

❑ Select the proper size of air conditioning unit for your space.

❑ Buy units with the Energy Star label.

❑ Change the filter every month in the summer months and a couple of times in the winter.

❑ Use proper R-Value insulation in the walls, in ceilings, and under the floors if you have a crawlspace or basement.

❑ Seal up cracks with caulk.

❑ Call a professional to clean the ducts or service your HVAC system.

15

INSULATION AND VENTILATION

When I was an apprentice carpenter in Local 608 in Manhattan, I worked with men who liked to bust my chops. The first time I worked with insulation I wore long sleeves, pants, boots, and gloves. Nevertheless, it got all over me. But the journeyman carpenter I was working with instructed me to go directly home after work and take a hot shower to get the fibers off my skin, and so I did. Unfortunately for me, hot water makes one's pores open, so the fiberglass was pushed deeper into my pores. Of course, this was the last time I listened to him! Please learn from my mistake: Wear long sleeves, pants, socks, goggles, and gloves. I like to tape my gloves to the cuffs of my shirt, and I always take a cool or cold shower after working with fiberglass, using a washcloth to scrub away the fibers from my skin.

In 2005, I worked on a show for The DIY Network called *Best Built Home*; it focused on making a home more comfortable, durable, efficient, healthy, and safe. To achieve this, a builder needs to focus on an integrated approach to building. There is a saying in construction: *build tight and ventilate right*. This means you seal up a home to make it airtight and prevent moisture from penetrating the building envelope, which is your home. Buttoning it up requires a builder to pay special attention to air-sealing using caulk and expandable foam to fill in any cracks or holes.

Once the home is sealed tight, it must have adequate insulation to keep the hot or cold air outside. Ventilation is equally important—a healthy home needs to breath. Moisture is the biggest enemy to a home since it can cause deterioration,

IN THIS CHAPTER

- Understanding R-Value
- Insulating your home
- Types of insulation
- Ventilating your home
- Proper attic ventilation
- Foundation vents

mold, and mildew. So, you need to deal with the moisture your home creates from cooking, bathing, and washing clothes. Ventilation is key. First, let's look at insulation.

INSULATION

Sealing cracks with caulk or expandable foam is the first step in insulating your home. Once your home has been sealed properly, make sure your walls, floors, and ceilings are properly insulated. By buttoning up your home, you will save a great deal of money on your utility bill, as well as create a more comfortable living environment.

Insulating the attic floor is very important when trying to keep your living space cool in the summer and warm in the winter. This will help keep your utility bill low all year. An insulated attic is also important in the winter because it prevents ice dams. When an attic is warm in the winter, the snow melts, creating ice on the roof, potentially breaking down the roof's materials, and ultimately letting water into the attic and the living space below.

R-Value

When you purchase insulation, you will notice it has different R-Values. You will also notice that the higher the R-Value, the thicker the insulation. R-Value is the measurement of a material's resistance to the passage of heat.

The Department of Energy has a chart for R-Values for existing houses on its website at http://www.eere.energy.gov/consumerinfo/energy_savers/r-value_map.html.

Once you figure out the correct R-Value number for your walls, ceilings, and floors, you can determine what type of insulation you will need.

Types of Insulation

If you have an older home, you may have loose-fill vermiculite or perlite insulation. This type of insulation is no longer used in construction. If your old insulation looks sparse or broken down, you can always go over the old insulation with new insulation without removing the old, as long as it is not wet, damp, or compromised.

Blanket Insulation

Blanket insulation is also known as *batt* or *rolls*. This type of insulation is cut in strips that fit between the floor joists, ceiling joists, or studs in the wall. This insulation also comes with a vapor barrier paper or reflective foil on one side. Always place the vapor barrier (the paper) face down against the living space area to keep the moisture produced in your home out of the attic. For instance, if you place blanket insulation in your attic to seal the ceiling below it, the insulation between the joists should have the paper facing down so you would see only the exposed insulation when standing in the attic (see Figure 15.1). If you put the insulation on the roof of the attic, you would see the paper side of the insulation facing you.

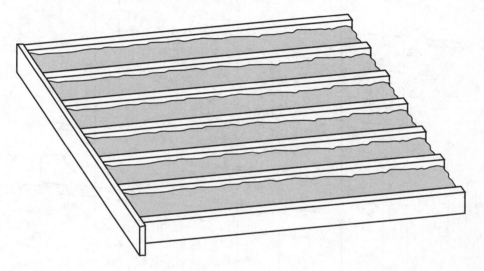

FIGURE 15.1

Batt insulation is laid between the joists.

Blanket insulation is used in unfinished walls; in floors; and in ceilings between studs, joists, and beams.

Loose-Fill Insulation

Loose-fill insulation is a popular choice in homes that already have the walls in place. Loose-fill insulation can be made of fiberglass, slag wool, or rock wool. If you are planning on using this in new construction, you must have netting stapled to the studs to hold the material in place. Loose-fill materials can be blown-in (see Figure 15.2) or sprayed. Sprayed mineral fiber usually has water or an adhesive to make it stick to the surface on which it is being sprayed.

Loose-fill insulation is used in enclosed existing wall cavities, unfinished attic floors, and hard-to-reach places. Installers drill a hole at the top of the wall between the studs and blow in the insulation until if fills the cavity.

FIGURE 15.2

Loose-fill insulation is blown in.

Rigid Insulation

Rigid insulation is also known as *extruded polystyrene foam (XPS), expanded poly-styrene foam (EPS), polyurethane foam,* and *polyisocyanurate foam.* Basically, it looks like dense foam and comes in sheets (see Figure 15.3).

Rigid insulation is often used in finishing basement walls. When using this inside your home, cover it with at least 1/2" drywall. Some rigid insulation comes with a foil facing to act as a vapor retarder. This insulation is used on the exteriors of homes with a weatherproof facing on the outside of it.

Expandable Foam Insulation

Expandable foam insulation is a wonderful choice to both insulate and seal your home. Expandable foam is used in new construction or renovations. Its installation is a job for professionals, who spray the foam and let it expand and set before they cut it flush to the face of the studs, joists, or beams. The upside to this is a tight seal and insulation. The downside is that it is very hard to run wires through the walls in the future.

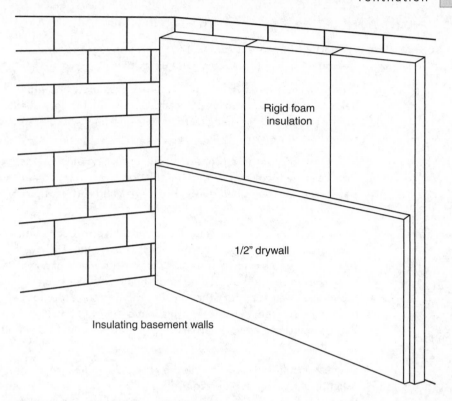

Rigid foam insulation

1/2" drywall

Insulating basement walls

FIGURE 15.3

Rigid insulation is often used in basement walls.

VENTILATION

A home needs to be able to breath properly to prevent mold, mildew, and water damage from trapped moisture. I am partial to whole-house fans that are installed in the attic and pull fresh air through open windows and screen doors. The breeze that is created with these fans is heavenly.

It's as necessary for the living space of your home to be ventilated as it is for the attic and crawlspace underneath your home to be properly ventilated. For this reason, proper attic ventilation and foundation vents are important. A hot attic is only going to penetrate the living space below and drive up your utility bill in the summer.

Attic Ventilation

Attic ventilation is important because it can extend the life of your roof and attic structure. It can also save you money in repair costs and utility bills.

> **TIP**
>
> If your attic requires more than R-Value 38, install two layers of batt insulation with the first layer's paper facing down and the second layer lying perpendicular to the first layer. Buy the second layer without the paper or vapor barrier on it. If you buy blanket insulation with the vapor paper on it for the second layer, make a series of slices in the paper so moisture will not get trapped between the two layers. Lay the second layer of insulation perpendicular to the first layer.

During warmer months, attics tend to get extremely hot. Ventilation helps keep the attic cool and therefore prevents the roof sheathing from warping and the shingles from deteriorating. A cooler attic can result in lower energy costs.

In the winter months, a properly ventilated attic helps reduce moisture, keeping the attic dry. Both ventilation and insulation help keep water from backing up underneath shingles and rotting the roof structure.

A balanced circulation system with equal intake through soffit vents and outtake through roof or gable vents is essential. The overhang of your roof creates a soffit. (The *soffit* is the underside of a roof overhang.) Vents should be installed underneath this overhang to help with the intake of air for your attic. If your attic is getting too hot but is properly insulated, consider putting in more soffit vents. For homes that have little to no soffit area, use a vented drip edge to ventilate your attic.

Because insulation is needed in the attic, use *baffles*, which are lightweight polystyrene molded to make a path for the air to flow up from the soffit. This way the insulation will not obstruct the soffit vents (see Figure 15.4).

You also want to direct air out of your attic. To do this, you should install various vents. A *gable vent* is located underneath the peak of your roof at one or both ends. You can install a fan at a gable vent to help remove hot air. A *roof vent* sits on top of the roof and either comes with a fan to help circulate the air or is a static vent that allows the air to move through it. *Turbines* are a nonelectric alternative to ventilation. They use air pressure and the force of the wind to spin the vanes of the turbine, pulling out the hot, humid, and stale air.

> **TIP**
>
> Use metal screens behind all vents to keep rodents and birds out of the attic.

A *continuous ridge vent* is a continuous vent at the top of your roof. It runs along the ridge and provides consistent ventilation because hot air always rises. Continuous ridge vents are usually installed during the construction of the home, but they can be retrofitted later if you are planning to install a new roof. The healthiest roof is one with soffit vents and a continuous ridge vent (see Figure 15.5).

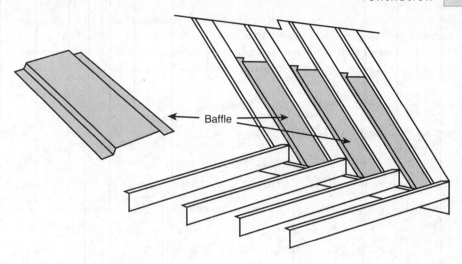

FIGURE 15.4

Air flows up through the soffit vents and through the baffles to circulate air in the attic.

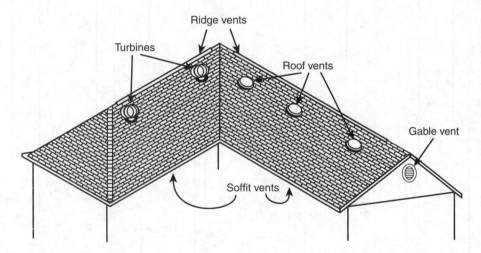

FIGURE 15.5

Various venting options include soffit, continuous ridge, gable, roof, and turbine vents.

Foundation Vents

Foundation vents are necessary to keep air flowing underneath your home to remove moisture from the crawlspace. Moisture can cause damp rot, which can deteriorate the wood and also create a great home for termites.

There are a few foundation vents to choose from: powered vents that have a fan attached to them, automatic vents that open and close according to the temperature, and manual vents that you have to open or close by hand depending on the season (you open the vents in the spring and close them in the fall or winter).

CHECKLIST

- ❑ Seal all cracks with caulk or expandable foam.

- ❑ Determine the proper R-Value for your area of the country.

- ❑ Insulate your attic, walls, and crawlspace with the proper insulation and R-Value.

- ❑ Ventilate your attic with soffit vents, ridge or roof vents, gable vents, and possibly fans.

- ❑ Use foundation vents to prevent termites and damp rot.

16

LANDSCAPE, YARD, AND GARDEN

I think one of the most miraculous gifts in life is to watch something grow. Whether it's a baby, one's hair, or a seedling, everything seems to have a genetic coding to move forward. After living in Manhattan, the land of steel and concrete, for more than 20 years, I was thrilled to set up an office in sunny California with palm trees, sculpted landscapes, and exotic flowers. What I have learned in Los Angeles is that it takes lots of TLC (and sometimes money) to keep your yard looking lush and gorgeous.

LANDSCAPE

When you purchase a home, it is important to check out the outside as well as the inside. The landscape can be broken down into two categories: the *hardscape* and the *softscape* (see Figure 16.1).

The hardscape consists of masonry work, such as stone walls, tile paths, brick or concrete patios, and fountains, and woodwork, such as decks, arbors, and planting boxes. You will start with the hardscaping first, which is the most labor-intensive part of landscaping. The softscape includes the animate or horticultural elements of the landscape, such as lawns, gardens, shrubs, and trees.

Many components make up a landscape, such as the slope of the land; the type of grass used; and various trees, shrubs, flowering plants, rocks, and ponds. The landscape of your property dictates the home's curb appeal and the flow of ground water. It is important that the landscape slope away from your home, if at all possible. If you have to live with a lawn sloping toward your home, you need to install a foundation drain or French drain to redirect the water from your home. For more information on drainage, refer to Chapter 6, "Drainage."

A well-designed and properly executed landscape design can increase your property's value. Conversely, a poorly conceived landscape design can decrease your property's value and waste your money and time—not to mention that it can be a liability if you do not consider drainage.

The basic elements to consider when landscaping include

- Color
- Form
- Line
- Scale
- Texture

Color

You may remember the color wheel or color theory from your art classes. The spectrum of color is divided into four categories:

- **Primary**—Red, yellow, and blue
- **Secondary**—Green, violet, and orange
- **Tertiary**—A mixture of primary and secondary colors
- **Neutral**—White, gray, and silver

Landscapers refer to this wheel when choosing colors to complement and unify your landscape. Many times warmer colors, such as red, orange, and yellow, are used together, or cooler colors, such as blue, green, and purple, are used together. It can be risky to use these two types of colors together, but many landscapers deliberately juxtapose colors to achieve a greater contrast. As you know from decorating the inside of your home, colors can influence your mood and the feel to your yard. Warm colors excite a person, whereas cool colors relax the viewer. Red is often used for focal points, and the cool colors are used for meditation areas.

Form

Form is a design term describing the shape of a plant such as upright, oval, spreading, weeping, or columnar. Ultimately, the shape of plants and trees affects the visual line.

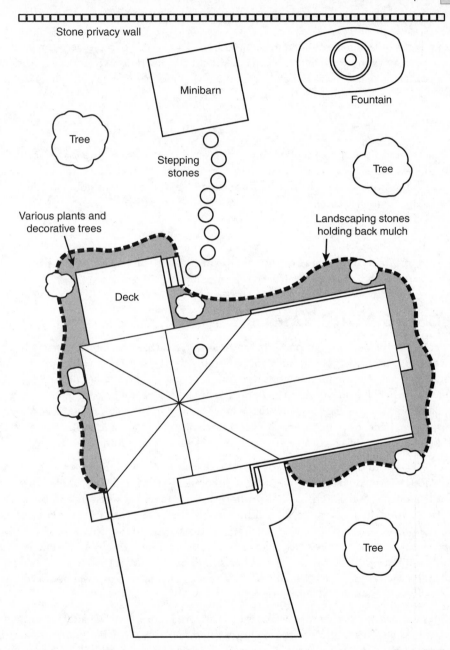

Stone privacy wall

Minibarn

Fountain

Tree

Stepping stones

Tree

Various plants and decorative trees

Landscaping stones holding back mulch

Deck

Tree

FIGURE 16.1

Stone walls, paths, fountains, arbors, and fences are examples of hardscaping. Trees and flower beds are examples of softscaping.

Line

Line refers to the general flow of the landscape to the viewer's eye across a landscape. The borders, plant groupings, and plants should all fit and flow together on vertical and horizontal planes. If it doesn't all fit together, whatever is out of place will pull away the viewer's focus and interrupt this flow.

Scale

Scale refers to the size of a plant, bush, or tree in relation to the buildings around it. If you have a large home, you will want large trees, but a smaller home would be dwarfed by such big trees. Always keep the proportion to the rest of your home in mind when designing your landscape.

Texture

Texture refers to the surface quality of a plant or tree. The bloom, too, is a big component to your landscape, giving it a coarse, medium, or fine look or feel.

DESIGNING YOUR YARD

Because of the various components that make up a successful landscape, many people hire a landscape designer to pull their vision together. Whether you hire out the job or tackle it yourself, you need to consider your lifestyle and how your yard will be used. Do you have children who are active outdoors? If so, you will need to plan a yard for sports and exercise. Do you entertain a lot, or plan to? Then you need to consider a large lawn, deck, or patio conducive to entertaining. Do you need a place to meditate? Then you may want to put in a koi pond or rock garden to soothe your nerves.

You will want to do your hardscaping first because it is labor intensive and needs to be in place before you decorate with the softscaping. Fences and walls should be thought out thoroughly. Make sure you know where your property line begins and ends. There is nothing worse than paying for a beautiful fence or stone wall to find out later that it sits on the property of a disgruntled neighbor, who asks you to move it! Just as you want to accentuate desirable views, you also want to block out unsightly views. Fences and walls can both provide privacy and act as sound barriers. Whether you delineate your property by a wood fence, stone wall, or a row of bushes or trees will be up to the overall need and unity of your property.

Walkways are made of stone, brick, or cement; are labor-intensive; and require a good bit of hauling. This is another reason you should make sure you get your hardscaping finished first. You don't want to tear up or kill any grass or plants while doing your project.

Gazebos, arbors, and decks offer nice focal points and entertaining spots in your yard. Water gardens, ponds, and fountains are also focal points that lend a relaxing feel to a yard. Because these areas are impressive on their own, minimal planting or softscaping is necessary. Water and rock gardens rely on rocks, stones, water, and wood to create a tranquil mood.

Lighting is a big consideration when designing your yard. The difference between your yard in the daylight and when it gets dark is like...night and day, literally! Nighttime can give the outdoors a magical and romantic feel, with the right lighting. Consider highlighting certain trees with spotlights and using low-lying solar lamps. Candlelight and torches add serenity and a romantic mood to a garden. (Always be careful when using candles or torches outdoors, though.) The type of atmosphere you would like to create will dictate your choice of lights. Chinese lanterns create a tranquil yet festive feel and would go well in a meditative garden, while Mexican candleholders fit into a southwestern theme.

Energy conservation and lowering your home's utility bill are important considerations when choosing trees. Deciduous trees planted in the south and west areas of a yard will serve as shade trees in the summer, lowering air conditioning costs. Because deciduous trees lose their foliage in the winter, they allow the warmth of the sun to filter into the home, thus helping heat it. The best-known deciduous trees produce fall foliage, with their leaves changing color from bright green to red, yellow, or orange.

Evergreen trees are what they sound like. They stay green year round and are planted to the north and west of a home to serve as windbreakers. Breaking the wind in the winter will lower your heating bill. Planting shrubs around the perimeter of your home—staying a few feet from the foundation—creates an insulating dead space around your home.

Always remember that tree limbs should never hang over your roof or touch your house. Untrimmed branches make it necessary to clean your gutters of leaves and debris more frequently. Leaves and dripping sap can ruin the look of your roof and also cause mold.

Flowering trees add an element of color and beauty to a yard. Fruit trees are both attractive and practical—the fruit can give a splash of color when the tree bears fruit. My lemon tree produces an abundant amount of lemons and adds a pretty, vibrant yellow to my yard.

When it is time to plant your garden, you have many choices, such as flowering plants, vegetables, or herbs. Flowering plants come in two types: annuals and perennials. *Perennials* come up each year, as long as the weather conditions remain optimal. These plants are economical since you pay for them once and can then enjoy them for years to come. You may think it would be foolish to buy *annuals*, which are flowering plants that live one season and then die. In fact, annuals have a lot of assets. For instance, it's easy to create an instant beautiful flower bed because you can buy the annuals already in bloom. The flowers on most annuals are usually brighter and more vivid than those on perennials. Perennials usually have less vibrant colors and their bloom times are shorter than annuals. An annual plant can also be clipped back and usually bloom all season long.

A vegetable garden is wonderful for its practical reasons, but it also yields beautiful plants such as kelp and cucumber vines that can be trained to climb up a trellis. Plant a vegetable garden in an area of your property that receives a good amount of sun. You will need to make sure your vegetable garden receives adequate water. Herb gardens can be beautiful to the eye and, let's face it, there is nothing like saving yourself a few dollars and plucking basil or dill out of your own garden.

Pruning

Trees and shrubs usually need to be pruned at certain times of the year when they are dormant. Flowering shrubs should be pruned after the flowers fade, although the shrubs that flower in late summer should be pruned in spring before they flower.

Thin out dead and misdirected branches, cutting to the base of the branch. Shape the branches by cutting just above a bud on the outside branches. In areas prone to fires, always clean away brush, trim your trees, and remove low-lying limbs.

Prune mature trees carefully and cut the branch to the stub, leaving a slight collar. Never cut a branch flush with the trunk or leave too much sticking out—you shouldn't be able to hang a hat on it. Prune hedges flat on the top and sides, flaring out toward the bottom to expose the base to the sun and encourage growth.

Grass

Planting grass can be overwhelming when it is time to choose the right kind of grass to buy. The type of grass you should buy is mandated by the area in which you live, how much traffic will be on the grass, and how much energy you will have for maintenance. Most grasses will go dormant with extended periods of draught.

Cool season grasses are for climates that have cold winters and hot summers. Usually these areas have regular rain storms in the summer months. Cool season grasses include Kentucky bluegrass, perennial ryegrass, and tall fescue. Transition zones are areas between the northern and southern regions, including the lower parts of Virginia and North Carolina, West Virginia, Tennessee, Kentucky, Arkansas, Ohio, Indiana, Illinois, Missouri, and Kansas. *Transition grasses* are a mixture of warm and cool season grasses, such as the various Kentucky bluegrasses and fescues. *Warm season grass* grows in the south and requires regular maintenance year round. These include Bahia, Bermuda, buffalo, carpet, centipede, and St. Augustine grass, to name a few. When the cooler weather approaches in the south, the grass may turn brown. Gardeners therefore use a technique called *winter seeding*, which involves planting ryegrass to keep the lawn looking green year round.

Fertilizer

Fertilizer adds nutrients and texture that is missing in the soil but is needed to support the trees, shrubs, flowers, vegetables, or herbs. First, you must know if your soil is acidic, alkaline, rich, weak, clay, or sandy. Soil test kits can be found in your local nursery or hardware store.

You can buy fertilizer in organic or chemical types that help nourish fruit or leafy trees and feed specific plants. Inorganic fertilizers are designed to help plants absorb nitrogen, potassium, and phosphorus. These elements should be in the soil, but some plants require more than is usually found in soil.

Nitrogen encourages the growth of stems and leaves by promoting chlorophyll and protein. When phosphorus is added, the plant or tree will produce more flowers, larger fruit, and healthier roots. Phosphorus also helps a plant to resist diseases. Potassium fosters protein development, thereby thickening stems and leaves.

Organic fertilizers such as manure, bat guano, compost, peat moss, and wood ash are all good additives for the soil since they have a long-term effect on the soil yet have lower concentrations of nutrients. This is the perfect choice for gardens and can improve the soil over a period of years. Because they gradually release nutrients, the plant can pick and choose which mineral benefits it over the entire growth cycle. Composting your organic waste is a great way to make your own organic fertilizer.

If you need to alter the pH level of your soil, you can use an inorganic fertilizer such as ammonium sulfate or aluminum sulfate to make the soil more acidic. Lime makes the soil more alkaline.

Mulch

Mulch helps to remove the threat of weeds, prevents the rapid evaporation of water, and adds texture to the overall design of your landscape. Various organic materials can be used as mulch. Cocoa bean shells offer a uniform color and fabulous smell. Pecan hulls also offer a uniform color and are great for small garden beds. Wood chips are good around trees, as paths, and around woody plants. Chopped up leaves also make a nice choice around trees or woody plants, and pine needles are perfect around acid-loving plants such as conifers, hollies, and rhododendrons.

Gravel is a nice choice for arid regions with cactus and rock gardens. River rocks can also be nice for such places but, when used in other regions, weeds can find their way up through the cracks.

Irrigation

When I was growing up in Atlanta, our irrigation system was an entertainment center. Our front hose connected to a sprinkler that went back and forth and provided my brother and me hours of fun. If we wanted our entire yard hit with water, we needed to move the sprinkler head. Of course, nowadays, there are very sophisticated sprinkler systems available, although they fall into two categories: sprinkler and drip (or trickle).

Figure 16.2 shows the two types of sprinkler heads in action.

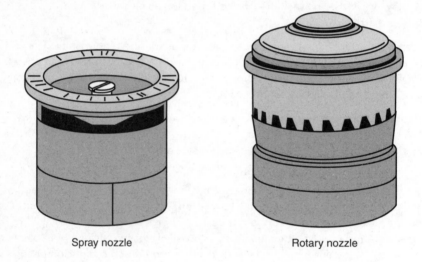

Spray nozzle   Rotary nozzle

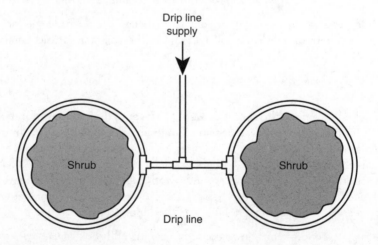

Drip line
supply

Shrub   Shrub

Drip line

FIGURE 16.2

Sprinkler system and drip irrigation are both effective ways to water your lawn and garden.

The *sprinkler system* can be as simple as I previously described, or it could be as complicated as an interlocking system underneath the soil. One factor that must be considered is ensuring that the number of sprinkler heads matches the pressure and volume of the water. Rotary and spray heads are the most common types of sprinklers used in lawns and gardens. Rotary heads can cover an area of 30–50 radius feet and require more water pressure than spray heads. Rotary heads are adjustable from a 20°–360° range. Spray heads, on the other hand, have a smaller radius of 10–20 feet. Spray heads are used in small, narrow, or unusually shaped areas. Spray heads are available in half circles, quarter circles, square patterns, and rectangular patterns to irrigate any area.

The *drip irrigation system* consists of a control station that controls the pressure and timing. The main lines direct the water from the control station to the emitters and lateral lines. The emitters decrease the water pressure to allow the water to emerge as droplets, and the lateral lines are either porous-wall tubing with small holes or individual units. This irrigation works well for row crops in vegetable gardens and closely spaced plantings.

Remember, anytime you set up an irrigation system, there is a trial-and-error period in which you will need to play around to get the right timing, pressure, and positioning to work together. Always configure your drainage system so your plants never get too much water.

CHECKLIST

❑ Spend time designing your landscape, taking into consideration color, form, line, scale, and texture to give your property the balance and unity you are trying to achieve.

❑ Be sure you know where you property line begins and ends.

❑ Choose lighting carefully to achieve the ambiance you want at night.

❑ Prune back trees to promote growth and remove excess fuel for brush fires.

❑ Choose grass that best fits your needs and area.

❑ Test your soil to ensure you choose the right fertilizer for your garden.

❑ Irrigate your plants, gardens, and trees to keep them healthy.

17

PAINTING

I remember watching my parents paint my bedroom my favorite color: pink! What amazed me was how much color could change my room. It was the '60s and I had a huge pink footprint rug, pink carpet, and a matching pink paisley desk organizer. You could say I was hip and happening. Well, at least I thought so.

I like to think that paint is to your home the way hair color and highlights are to your hair. It's amazing what a thin layer of paint can do for your home, both on the inside and outside. How long a layer of paint lasts will depend on the type of paint, the quality, the finish you use, and what you do in your home. For instance, in a home with a smoker who smokes inside the home, in time the paint will have a layer of tar on it. If the finish can be wiped down, then the paint color can last longer, but if it is a flat paint, it will look yellow in a matter of a few of years.

I painted my entire home a couple of years ago. Some rooms look like I painted a month ago, while others look like they could use another coat or at least some touchups here and there. There are certain areas that have more traffic and the walls surrounding them have marks and nicks. The molding around the doorways and the base molding also are showing some wear and tear from furniture hitting them, the vacuum cleaner bumping them, and oils from hands. On the other hand, my Manhattan apartment still has the original faux finish on the walls, which is over 10 years old. In general, interior paint will last 5-10 years and exterior paint will last 7-10 years.

Chapter 17 | Painting

There are certain areas that you should not skimp on, and paint is one of them. The better the paint you buy, the longer it will last. Also, the better the paint, the easier it will be to apply. Before you buy paint, check out the manufacturer's website. Most manufacturers have lots of great tips and online tools to calculate how much paint you will need to buy for your room.

Preparation

Before you do any painting, always make sure you take the time to prep the room. This is the hardest part of painting, but it will result in a job you can be proud of. Use dropcloths over floors and furniture, and tape hardware such as door handles, locks, and hinges. Fill in cracks, gouges, and holes with joint compound or spackle (see Figure 17.1). Always make sure you prime over any spackle before painting the room.

Primer/Sealer

There are companies that make primers and sealers out of latex, oil/alkyd, or a shellac. It is always good to read the label to see which primer is best for your use. My personal favorite sealer and primer is the shellac-based primer with a white pigment. I have found this to be the best to cover any stain so it will not bleed through your new paint. Remember, primer does not "seal" any stains—it just primes the walls. If you want to paint over an existing paint, then I would suggest you use a primer and tint it the color of the finish paint. If you are painting over a stain or trying to cover up smoke discoloration or musty odors, I would use the shellac sealer/primer because it seals and primes.

Color

Color can be such a remarkable change in a room. It can also act as an optical illusion. For instance, if you put a dark paint on the ceiling, it will make the ceiling feel lower. Most people use a white or very light color paint for the ceiling for this very reason.

When it comes time to pick out the color of your room, unless you are an innate interior designer, you might want to browse through design magazines. It's a good idea to figure out the entire scheme of the room before you paint. Once you get the rugs, wallpaper, and fabrics picked out, you'll have plenty of colors of paint to choose from.

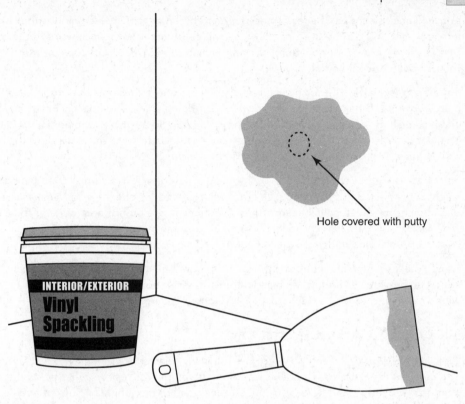

Hole covered with putty

FIGURE 17.1

Spackle over all holes, let them dry, and sand them smooth.

If you want to try a bold color in a room, try buying a quart can of paint and painting one wall first to see if it looks as good in person as it does in your mind.

Flat, Satin, Eggshell, Semigloss, or Glossy Finish

Flat paint is typically used on the ceilings of most rooms except the bathroom and kitchen. It is also used throughout a home since it has a matte finish that will not reflect light; therefore, it will hide imperfections such as bumps and cracks easier than a paint with sheen to it. Flat enamel is becoming more popular because it has a matte finish yet can handle the occasional wiping.

TIP

If there's a color that you like but you cannot find it in the paint swatches, you can bring in the color from a piece of fabric or from a magazine and most paint stores can mix up the color exactly.

Eggshell has the sheen of guess what? That's right, an eggshell! This paint is popular for interior walls and can be used on all walls. This finish can be wiped down, and the moisture in the bathroom from bathing or the steam in the kitchen from cooking won't stain the paint like it would a flat.

Satin paint is my favorite for highly trafficked areas and bathrooms that don't have too much moisture. It has a velvety sheen without it being shiny. The finish is between a flat and a semigloss. You can wipe it down and it can handle a light scrubbing. This would be a good choice in a child's room where you may need to wipe the walls down from spilled juice or dirty handprints.

Semigloss is a great choice for the bathroom and kitchen. It has a finish that can handle a light scrubbing. Semigloss and high gloss will reflect a lot of light, which makes them bad choices for most walls because they will show all the bumps and joints of the drywall. Along with bathrooms and kitchens, semigloss makes an excellent finish for moldings, doors, wainscoting, and other decorative designs since it has a subtle shine.

Glossy makes a nice choice for moldings and doors because its sheen is very shiny. However, because of that, it will highlight any imperfection on your surface. It is easily wiped down and tends to stay looking good longer than other finishes.

Latex, Oil, and Alkyd Paint

Typically, house paint is composed of the following: pigment, a binder, and a solvent. The *pigment* is what gives the paint its color. The *binder*, or *resin*, is what holds the paint itself together and holds it to the surface you are painting. The *solvent* acts as a thinning agent. Today's paints have even more additives to help achieve certain goals, such as speeding up drying time and inhibiting mold.

Latex paint has been an absolute joy for those of us who are do-it-yourselfers. Latex paint has come a long way in the past 20 years and is just as good as oil paint for most applications. It is a versatile paint that bonds to drywall, wood, plaster, aluminum, some plastics, masonry, and galvanized metal. Latex is much easier to clean up because it is water soluble, making it environmentally friendly.

Natural latex used to be the resin in early latex paint. Now you will find acrylic to be the resin in latex paint. *Latex acrylic* has become quite popular since acrylic has a chemical composition that allows the paint to expand and contract with the temperature. Because of this, latex acrylic will hold a little better and last a bit longer. This is a very popular exterior paint.

Oil paints were made of natural oils, such as linseed oil and tung oil, and turpentine, which is a solvent. *Alkyd* paints have mostly replaced oil paints and use a synthetic resin called *alkyd*, with mineral spirits as their solvent. Alkyd paints can be used on more surfaces than oil paints. Oil and alkyd paint require caustic solvents to clean it up, making them less environmentally friendly than latex. If rags are not stored properly with oil paint, they can self-combust and have been the reason for many a fire in homes. Some paints combine both oil and alkyd; however, when people refer to paint, they usually divide them into latex or oil.

Stains

Stains are different from paints since they do not completely cover the surface to which they are applied. However, much like paint, stains come in oil-based or water-based form. The good news/bad news with water-based stains is that they dry quickly. If you need time to work with a stain, then you may want to consider an oil-based stain.

PAINTING THE ROOM

After you have patched and primed the walls, now you can start to paint. Move your furniture away from the walls and into the middle of the room with plastic or a drop-cloth over them.

Paint your ceiling first. I like to cut in the corners first and then roll out the ceiling. Do the same with the walls. *Cutting in* refers to the tedious task of applying paint to the edges where the wall meets the door casing, molding, ceiling, and baseboards (see Figure 17.2). I cut in around the doors, base molding, and other moldings first; then I roll out the paint. I suggest you paint the trim last. Make sure you buy a nice tapered paint-brush to cut in at the corners.

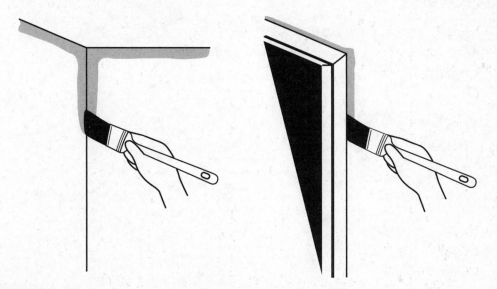

FIGURE 17.2

Use a tapered paint brush to cut in around moldings and where the wall meets the ceiling.

Paint Removal

Paint removal can be a real pain. Many people want to remove paint from old moldings and then replace the paint with a stain. This can be a time-consuming job. There are many products on the market that will remove paint. I suggest you buy the ones that are not caustic to the environment and your skin. Always look for the manufacturer's instructions and protect your eyes and skin when removing paint.

Lead Paint

Lead paint removal has become a big business since lead-based paint has caused lead poisoning in many children and lead poisoning can lead to severe brain damage. You can pick up a lead paint testing kit at your hardware store.

Tip

You can buy a lead paint test kit at your hardware store.

If your home has lead paint, you can remove and replace items such as doors and windows. You can also cover the paint with a major sealant or cover it with drywall. The other choice is to have it removed by professionals.

In most cases, if you have lead paint, so do the people who live nearby. Ask your neighbors how they handled the lead paint in their homes. You might get a good recommendation for a contractor.

Checklist

❑ Take the time to prepare your room for paint.

❑ Always use a primer/sealer over spackle or stains.

❑ Determine the best finish for your room.

❑ Choose the fabrics and furniture before you paint your room.

❑ Properly store and dispose of oily rags.

❑ Always protect your eyes and skin when painting and removing paint.

❑ Hire a professional to remove lead paint.

18

PLUMBING

Of all the trades, the plumbers seem to get the bum wrap...ehem...so to speak. I'm not exactly sure why because, when a home has a major leak or a sewage problem, plumbers suddenly become our superheros!

The first time I tried my hand at plumbing I installed a stackable washing machine. I feel sorry for the poor guys at my hardware store who tried to understand me needing the "doohickey" that connects to the "thingamajig." Well, I've come a long way since then and have grown to really love how linear plumbing is. One pipe connects to the other and so on. The first thing you need to know is where water comes into your home and where it goes out.

There are couple ways that you receive water in your home. You may get it from the county you live in and pay for it, or you may be lucky enough to have a private well drilled down to the water table below your property. This is cost-effective as long as the water is drinkable. Some people have both systems and use the well water for watering their grass and plants.

Reservoirs capture water from rain, rivers, lakes, and underground water sources. Then the water is treated at treatment facilities before it reaches your home. These facilities keep a close check on the quality of the water.

IN THIS CHAPTER

- Knowing the differences between town water or private wells

- Testing the water in your private well

- Treating a contaminated well

- Understanding the plumbing system and pipes in your home

- Knowing the various pipes used for a home's plumbing

- Troubleshooting clogs and leaky faucets

- Troubleshooting a hot water heater

PRIVATE WELLS

If you have a private well, you must have it checked regularly for bacteria and arsenic. Bacteria can be either good or bad, and it is found in the upper soil layers, streams, ponds, and lakes. Septic systems that have broken down can also be a source of harmful bacteria such as e. coli, which is a coli form bacteria. Most bacteria is filtered out through the soil before it reaches the water table, but if the geology allows rapid absorption and movement of water to the water table, the well can be susceptible to harmful bacteria. Other concerns are viruses and protozoa, which usually get caught in the soil layers on the way down to the water table. This is why your well should be checked regularly.

Bacteria testing kits are available and affordable. A bacteriological analysis by a certified lab can cost about twice as much as the kits, and if a technician visits your home, the testing fee is likely to be higher. Contact your county's health department or a state agency for certified water laboratories and ask what kits they recommend.

When sampling water, follow the directions on the kit or from the laboratory. These directions usually include the following steps:

1. Use a sterile bottle and do not rinse.

2. Write your name, your address, and the date of sampling on the bottle.

3. Remove the aeration device from the faucet.

4. Run cold water for 3 minutes from the faucet closest to the well.

5. Reduce the water to a trickle for 1 minute.

6. Fill the bottle as directed and seal it tightly.

7. Keep the bottle cool.

8. Deliver the bottle to the lab immediately.

If you do find contamination in the water, you will need to disinfect the well. This process might need to be done two or three times to remove all the bacteria. Some wells may need a shock disinfection to keep the problem under control. State and county codes will tell you exactly what you need to do. For many years, well owners have used an economical solution of chlorine and water. A ratio of 1:100 is recommended (1 gallon of bleach to 100 gallons of water). Make sure you check with your state or county to make sure you use the proper product they suggest.

NOTE

For information, regulations, and guidelines, call the EPA Drinking Water Hotline at 800-426-4791.

Once you have put the disinfecting solution in your well, run your home's hose in the well and turn the water on for about 15–20 minutes to circulate the water. Run each of the faucets in the home until you smell chlorine; then turn them off. Leave the chlorinated water in the well for 24 hours, remove the chlorine water, and dispose of it as suggested by your county or state. Many times at a ratio of 1:100 the chlorinated water can go directly down the drain. Remove the water until the smell of chlorine is gone. Sample the water a day or two later and test it again.

Filtration systems are good to have but might not be able to remove all the bacteria. Change the filters regularly. Ultraviolet light is also used to remove bacteria; various UV lamp systems are available in which the water passes through the light, killing the bacteria. My favorite way to treat water is through an ozone generator because it is more effective than chlorine and doesn't use chemicals. The ozonation equipment and the operating costs are higher than other water treatment procedures, however.

Dig a well deep enough and use a casing or liner that is properly sealed so bacteria, protozoa, and viruses cannot leak down into the well.

THE PLUMBING SYSTEM IN YOUR HOME

If your water comes from the town you live in, you must pay for it. A water meter is installed so the town can keep track of how much water you use. Meters are installed outside the home in warm climates and inside the home in colder climates.

The pipe that brings the water into your home—whether it is from the city or your private well—is called the *main supply line*. This supply line passes through the water meter and then enters your home; the main shutoff valve is usually found near the home's entrance. This is an important valve because, if anything goes wrong with your plumbing system, you can turn off the entire water supply at the main shutoff valve. The main supply line passes this shutoff valve and has a t-joint, allowing a branch line to come off of it (usually vertically) to fill the water heater while the rest of the line feeds all the cold water into your home (including into sinks, toilets, the washing machine, and the dishwasher). This branch line feeds the cold water to the hot water heater; once the water is heated, another pipe directs it to the various fixtures and appliances that need hot water.

Figure 18.1 shows a typical plumbing system.

These fixtures, except the toilet, have hot and cold water feeding them and therefore require a drain line or waste pipe to remove the used water to the sewer line. This waste water uses gravity to flow to the sewer or septic tank, but for it to work properly, these pipes need air for the gravity to move the water. If there wasn't air in the waste pipes, a vacuum would be created and the water would just sit in place. For this reason, vent stacks are used near all fixtures (sinks, toilets, bathtubs, dishwashers, and washing machines). Vent pipes are nothing more than pipes that are spliced vertically in the waste pipes and that travel to a vent system that eventually leads to the roof via a main pipe called a *vent stack*. When it comes out of the roof, it is known as the *roof vent*. Now you know these pipes sticking up through your roof are for.

> **TIP**
>
> It's a good idea to put a small vent screen on top of your roof vent so leaves and debris do not get into the vents.

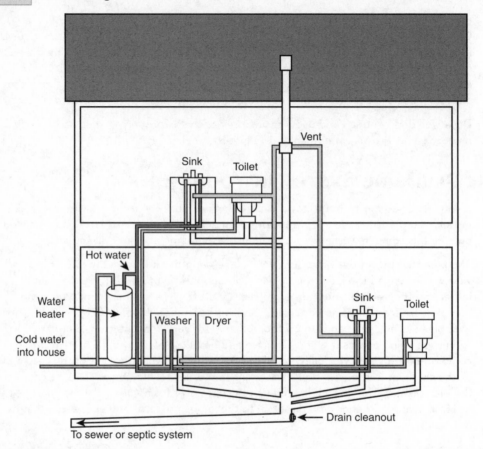

FIGURE 18.1

The ins and outs of your home's plumbing.

A drain cleanout is found at the end of the waste line of your home. Oftentimes, this cleanout is found outside the home, in the basement, or in the crawlspace. The plug to the cleanout usually has a square fitting that can be removed with an open-ended wrench or plumber's pliers.

PIPE MATERIALS

Your area's building codes will determine what you can use in your area. The available types of pipes are copper and rigid plastic such as ABS for drain lines; PVC for drain, vent, and cold water lines; and CPVC for both hot and cold water supply lines. The best piping to use is copper pipe since it lasts longer, but it requires soldering all joints and connections so installation is time-consuming and usually best left to a professional. Rigid plastic is easier for the do-it-yourselfer to install. I don't like to recommend mixing pipe materials because the weaker one will start to leak and many building codes will not permit it.

Be sure to insulate your pipes with pipe insulation, which comes in long tubes and slips over the pipes, and seal the seams with duct tape. Turn off the water to your outdoor spigot in the winter and be sure to drain the water after you shut down the valve. Use heat tape or heated cable around pipes that are susceptible to freezing. Using silicone caulk or insulating foam, seal all openings around pipes that may let in cold air.

Thaw a frozen copper pipe with a propane torch, hairdryer, or heat lamp. For PVC or CPVC, be sure to use a hairdryer. Keep the faucet open so steam doesn't get trapped and burst the pipe. Work from the faucet to the frozen area.

Plumbing Maintenance

Even for those who never ever want to understand plumbing, please read this section carefully because, for some reason (probably Murphy's Law), our toilets and sinks seem to clog, overflow, and break during a holiday or when we are trying to impress our in-laws. For this reason, it is important to be armed with a little know-how in cases of emergencies during times when you can't get a plumber over right away.

Water can cause an amazing amount of damage over time if the leak is coming from underneath a fixture. Mold and mildew develop quickly if the water and moisture are not dealt with quickly. Therefore, always fix a leaky faucet or a running toilet immediately! Recently, I fixed a running toilet that cost the homeowner an extra $350 a month in her water bill. It took me 10 minutes to replace the fill valve that cost $9!

Clogs

When your sink, toilet, or bathtub has clogged, it can be a bit daunting if you don't understand the basics of clogs. Most clogs are caused by food, hair, or grease buildup in a waste line. Sometimes an object or toy can get into the drain line and cause a clog. If you have an obstruction in your venting system, it can cause a clog or slow drainage, but this is rarely the case so always tackle a clog in the drain first.

A plunger is an inexpensive purchase that can produce great results in a clogged drain. Make sure you have some water on the bottom of the drain to form a seal around the plunger

Tip

The most important thing to know about a toilet is where the shut-off valve is. If your toilet is clogged and starting to overflow, reach down and turn off the shutoff valve at the back of the toilet that feeds it cold water. This will immediately stop the toilet from overflowing.

Chapter 18 Plumbing

before you start to pump the plunger. Give it about 8–10 tries. If that doesn't do the trick, try a drain cleaner or a plumber's snake.

Try using a home remedy drain cleaner first before you resort to a caustic commercial drain cleaner. Remember that everything you put down the drain goes into our environment. Heavy-duty cleaners are fairly toxic and can break down the bacteria in your septic system and eventually leak down into the water table. Heat a cup of white vinegar, pour the vinegar down the drain, and then add a few tablespoons of baking soda. This mixture will start to foam up. When the foaming stops, flush with hot water.

Check the P-trap by placing a bucket underneath it and loosening the fitting until it comes off. Check to see if an object has lodged in the bend. If that's not where the problem is, remove the P-trap so you can use a plumber's snake directly in the drain line.

Every home should have a *plumber's snake*, which looks like a disc-shaped gun with a pistol grip and a flexible ribbed cable that extends from the end of it. The spiral coil grabs the hair or object or cuts through the grease when the snake is pushed into the drain line and turned (see Figure 18.2). Remove the P-trap to easily push the plumber's snake into the drain line.

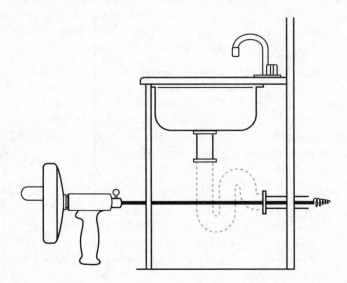

FIGURE 18.2

Use a plumber's snake directly in the drain line to remove a clog.

If this doesn't fix the clog, pick up the phone and call your plumber. She or he may need to use a huge snake called a power auger in your drain's cleanout, located either outside the home or in the basement or crawlspace, to remove debris from the waste line on the outside of your home. In some areas of the country, clay pipes are used for waste pipes. These pipes can crack, allowing the roots of trees and shrubs to get into the pipes and obstruct waste from moving through the pipe.

Leaky Faucets

Most faucet leaks can easily be fixed with a rubber washer, an O-ring, or seals—depending on the type of faucet. By fixing the problem yourself, you can save a good bit of money since plumbers can be expensive and will charge you a standard fee even if it takes only 10 minutes to fix the problem. For detailed information on various fixes, buy a general home repair book, such as *Lynda Lyday's Do It Yourself!*

Water Hammer

Water hammer is that loud noise you hear when you turn off a faucet, when the washing machine turns off, or when any other fixture turns off the water. Shutting off the flow of water can suddenly send a pressure wave down the water line, creating a sudden "hammer" noise. This sudden shock can eventually rupture copper pipes and cause leaks at the joints.

You can have a plumber install a *water hammer arrester*, which is an air chamber that cushions this pressure. These are usually installed in the area of the problem, but they can be installed in various places in the pipes, such as in the wall or just above a shut-off valve.

Toilets

A toilet has various components that break down but that can be easily and cheaply replaced. A fill valve assembly and flapper are the two most frequently replaced items in the toilet's tank. When they break down, they cause constant running water in the tank. A fill valve, flapper, float ball, or chain can be replaced for relatively little money. Always follow the instructions on the packaging.

A *toilet auger* (also known as a *closet auger* or *toilet snake*) is different from a plumber's snake and is helpful when there is an obstruction in the toilet. The toilet auger has a bent tip that fits easily into the toilet's built-in trap.

Hot Water Heater

Water heaters are heated by either gas or electricity. A gas heater has a gas burner that heats the tank from the bottom. An electric heater has two heating elements sticking into the tank from the side, heating the water.

Water heaters are insulated on the inside and outside of the tank. A heavy-duty steel tank holds the water and usually has a glass liner to keep rust out of the water. Various components make up a hot water heater. A dip tube feeds the tank with cold water, and a hot water pipe lets out the hot water and feeds it to various fixtures in your home. A control valve or thermostat controls the temperature or the gas burner, and a drain valve allows the tank to drain to remove sediment or when replacing the heating elements. A pressure relief valve keeps the tank from exploding if it gets too hot; a sacrificial anode rod helps prevent the steel in the tank from eroding. Figure 18.3 shows the typical components of an electric water heater.

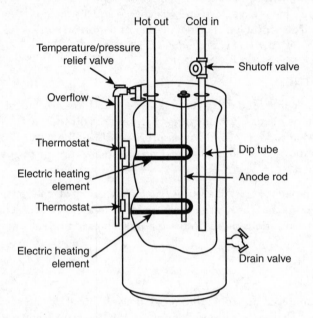

FIGURE 18.3

The typical components of a water heater.

Do the following to troubleshoot your hot water heater:

- Check the thermostat to make sure it hasn't gotten bumped up or down.

- Turn down the temperature when going on vacation so you won't spend money heating a tank that is unused. Remember to turn it back up upon your return.

- Replace the sacrificial anode rod when you see rust in your water supply. This can be unscrewed from the top and replaced with an anode rod that fits your appliance.

- If you do not have hot water in an electric hot water tank, read your water heater's manual for the proper procedure to check the heating elements with a multimeter.

- Replace the heating elements when needed. First, turn off the power to the water heater at the breaker box and turn off the main supply valve that feeds the tank. Drain the water below the heating elements through a hose attached to the drain valve. Remove the element(s) by unscrewing the mounting bolt. Usually a heating element that needs to be replaced has a break in the loop; replace it. Turn the water and power back on.

- Drain the tank to remove sediment, following the manufacturer's directions.

- For gas heaters that are not working properly, check to see if the pilot light is on. Make sure there is not a draft blowing it out.

- Check the dip tube to make sure cold water is getting to the bottom of the tank. Turn off the water to the tank, remove the dip tube, and replace it if it's broken.

Keep an eye on your water heater after 10 years because most hot water heaters need to be replaced after 10–15 years of use.

CHECKLIST

- ❏ Properly line a private well to keep bacteria, viruses, and protozoa from entering it.

- ❏ Check your well at least once a year.

- ❏ Treat your well if you have contamination using the products suggested by your area's health department.

- ❏ Insulate pipes properly so they don't freeze or burst.

- ❏ Keep a plunger and plumber's snake handy to remove clogs in your pipes.

- ❏ Try to avoid using commercial drain cleaners.

- ❏ Fix a leaky faucet easily with inexpensive replacement parts.

- ❏ Turn off the valve behind the toilet if it starts to overflow.

- ❏ Check an electric water heater's anode rods and heating elements and replace them when necessary.

19

Pools and Hot Tubs

I've always been a "water bug," as my father used to call me. From the moment I was introduced to water, I loved it. Oceans, lakes, rivers, and pools were always on my list of summer fun.

Those of you who have a pool or who grew up with one know that there is nothing like walking out your door on a hot summer day and taking a swim. We didn't have a pool growing up; instead our family was a member of a pool club. For me, the Olympic-size pool at the end of our street was heaven and where I learned how to swim. Eventually, I swam on a team—mostly for the new bathing suits and the powdered Jell-O we would ingest before a swim meet, thinking it had magic energy. Had I known at the time I was hypoglycemic, I would have figured out why; when it was time for me to get on the block and race, I wanted to curl up on a lounge chair and nap.

I remember the lifeguards very well. They had the lifeguard "whistle spin" down to a science. (If memory serves me correctly, I think it takes five spins for the whistle to hug tightly against the spinning finger.) The lifeguards also had the job of maintaining a huge pool with lots of children and adults.

Pool Maintenance

There are a few things you will need to do on a regular basis:

- Check the pH levels.
- Sanitize the pool from bacteria.
- Use an algae inhibitor.
- Sanitize the pool by shocking it.

- Add an inch of water when you service your pool.

- Use a tile soap down the middle of the pool to push scum to the sides.

- Clean the tile or side of the lining with a soft brush.

- Vacuum the pool.

Daily Maintenance

Be sure to do the following every day:

- Run the filter at least 8–10 hours daily, although 24 hours is best. Always run it during daylight hours.

- Remove floating debris.

- Clean the skimmer baskets.

- Use chlorine or nonchlorine chemicals as needed in an automatic dispenser or by putting tablets in the skimmers once a week. Floaters are also used that hold slow-dissolving tablets and remain in the pool at all times.

Testing pH Levels

A water's pH level is the measurement of the balance of acid and alkalinity. The scale ranges from 0 to 14, with 0 being extreme acidity and 14 being extreme alkalinity. A swimming pool needs to have the right balance of acidity and alkaline (a pH value between 7.2 and 7.6) for it to be comfortable to swim in and to keep the mechanics of the system working properly. You will become a chemist in no time trying to figure out the right amounts to bring the water to its proper pH level.

pH test kits are extremely user friendly since all you need to do is stick a test strip of paper in the water, wait for the paper to turn a color, and then match the color to the color chart that comes with the kit. This will tell you if your water needs more acid or alkaline.

An acidic reading will give you a darker color on the test strip and requires a pH increaser (muriatic acid or sodium bisulfate), which can be bought at pool equipment stores. Acidic water is uncomfortable to swim in because it causes your eyes to burn. In addition, it will eventually eat away the pool's filtration and pump system since it eats away at rubber and metal and corrodes metal.

An alkaline reading will give you a lighter color on the test strip and requires a pH decreaser (soda ash). Alkaline water won't burn your eyes, but it will leave your skin feeling dry and looking a bit chalky. The water itself will be cloudy and cause scaling to form on everything it contacts. Again, this can break down your equipment if not brought to the proper level.

Besides a pH testing kit, you should also get a sanitizer kit. This kit will show you how much bacteria is in your pool. The sanitizers come in a tablet or a stick that is put in a container near the filter and pump system.

You should also use an algae inhibitor in your skimmer to prevent more than 15,000 types of algae from getting started in your pool.

Shocking Your Pool

When you think of a public pool and all the people who swim in it, it can be fairly frightening to think of all the mucus, dead skin cells, cosmetics, suntan lotion, body oils, sweat, and body waste that can get into a pool. Which reminds me of a saying I once saw at a pool club: "There is no *P* in S-W-I-M-M-I-N-G. Let's keep it that way."

> **TIP**
>
> Pool dealerships usually have a water test facility. Bring in a sample of your pool water for a computer analysis. Often, the company you bought the pool from will do this free.

Now that I have scared you out of the water, I will try to coax you back in by informing you that there is a way to *shock* your pool, which is basically a chemical process known as *oxidation* that breaks down waste that is water-soluble. When shocking your pool, always use the right treatment for your pool. Typically, most people think of using chlorine to sanitize a pool, but there are other, nonchlorinated ways to treat the water. There are various chemicals you can use for a nonchlorinated system, such as bromide, which is easier on your skin and mucous membranes. You should shock a chlorinated pool with a chlorinated treatment.

The shocking chemicals are also known as *burners* and *oxidizers*. Most chemicals are put in the deep end of the pool and are fast dissolving. A pool skimmer is an excellent way to mix and distribute these chemicals and expedite the process. Always follow the manufacturer's instructions and use the right amount for your size pool.

How often you need to shock your pool will depend on usage. Some people shock their pools every two weeks. Always shock it at the start of the season and at least midway through.

Water Levels

Add an inch of water every time you service your pool to keep up with normal evaporation, usually once a week to keep the pool filled to the right level. If you wait weeks to do this, it will take hours to fill up your pool and you might forget to turn off the hose.

> **TIP**
>
> If you live in an area that experiences heavy rainstorms or hurricanes, always lower the water level of your pool before extreme storms hit. Find out how much water is expected to land in your area and drain the water in your pool that many inches. You do not want your pool to cause flooding in your home.

Cleaning Your Pool

Most people who have a pool cover tend to use it only when they're gone on vacation and during storms. The day-to-day debris that falls into the swimming pool should be dealt with daily. Use a telepole with a screen basket on the end of it to remove debris and leaves. Always clean out the skimmer baskets, too.

Use a tile soap by squirting it in the middle of the pool to push the pool's top scum to the sides, making it easier to float in the skimmer baskets or remove it with a vacuum or a screen basket. Brushing removes algae from the surface of the sides and bottom of the pool. When brushing the sides of the pool, always work from the top down and start at the shallow end, pushing the grime toward the main drain. If you have a pool with a liner, you will need to make sure you are very careful when cleaning it so you do not rip the liner. Always work from the top down, cleaning the top tiles first.

There are various types of vacuums you can get. The easiest are the automatic vacuums that do the work themselves. The electric robot is an expensive automatic pool cleaner and is most common in large pools. It is battery-operated and scans the bottom of the pool's floor, catching debris in a bag attached to it. The booster-type vacuum is also automatic and uses a pump and motor to send a pressurized stream of water into a catch bag, creating a vacuum while it patrols the bottom. The least-desirable option is the boosterless vacuum because you cannot heat and filter the pool at the same time. This unit uses the circulation pump to create the vacuum and attaches to the return line after the pump but before the filter. These units need an automated valve to control the system so that the heater doesn't turn on when cleaning.

To manually clean your pool, attach the head of your vacuum to the telepole and to the hose. Work your way down the sides and along the bottom, making sure you are moving slowly enough to pick up the dirt—rather than just moving it around. When you notice that the suction is weak, empty the strainer basket or clean the filter.

Heating a Pool

As with anything, the more you add onto a system, the more it will cost and the more repairs you may have down the line. But let's face it, a heated pool is a luxury.

There are three choices you have for heating a pool: solar, heat pump, and gas. Solar is the least expensive way to heat a pool and can last about 20 years with a warranty usually for 10 years. The most common way is a heat pump that uses electricity; it can last from 5–10 years with a warranty of 1–10 years. The most expensive way is a gas heater that heats your pool quickly, but it will last only about 5 years and has a warranty of 1–5 years.

Getting the Pool Ready for the Season

Do the following to get your pool ready for the season:

- Remove the cover. If you have a good bit of murky water on your cover, you may want to buy a submersible pump to remove the water. This can take a few days. Use your skimmer pole to remove leaves from the middle of the cover.

- Check the pump and clean out the leaf basket.

- Check the filter. Hopefully, you drained the filter at the end of last season. If not, you may have a good bit of grime and ick. You might need to change the filter media every 3 years. Pool filters come in three types: cartridges that are easily removed and replaced, diatomaceous earth, and sand filters. Diatomaceous earth (DE) is composed of pourous fossilized skeltons called *diatoms* that come in a powder form. These diatoms act as a filter medium that can be cleaned or replaced. The sand in sand filters can be scooped out and replaced. Always follow the manufacturer's directions. Figure 19.1 shows several kinds of pool filters.

> **TIP**
>
> Clean the pool cover by scrubbing it down with a soft pool brush on a telepole, rinsing it, and then letting it dry. Then sprinkle the cover with talcum powder, roll it up, and store it in a dry place. This way it will be easy to unroll it at the end of the season.

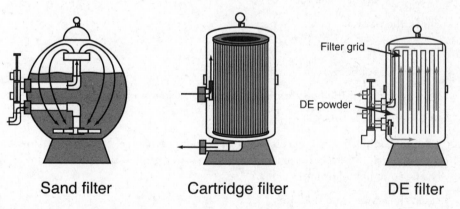

| Sand filter | Cartridge filter | DE filter |

FIGURE 19.1

Types of filters: sand filter, cartridge filter, and DE filter.

- Fill the water so it just enters the skimmers, which is usually 3"–6" from the top.

- Remove the leaves and debris from the bottom of the pool with the skimmer pole.

- Turn on the filter and the pump continuously for a few days.

- Remove algae by brushing the sides and bottom of the pool.

- Shut down the filtering system overnight and vacuum any algae on the bottom. Then turn on the filter again.

- A few days after your pool has been filled, check the chlorine or nonchlorine levels. You may need to shock the pool again if the water was really murky to begin with. A well-cared-for pool should only need one shock to get it ready.

- Add the algaecide.

- Make sure the pH level is between 7.2 and 7.6.

- Check the chlorine level.

This should take a few days before you are ready to play Marco Polo.

Closing the Pool

When the temperature outside gets to be reliably in the 40s at night and the high 60s to low 70s in the day, it's time to close your pool. If you close the pool down too early, then you are risking having the perfect climate for algae to grow. If you wait too long, then you are risking a heap of leaves in the pool. To close your pool, do the following:

- Bring the pH level to between 7.2 and 7.6.

- Remove any debris floating on the top of the water.

- Vacuum and brush the pool.

- Shock the pool.

- Add algaecide.

- Drain the pool below the skimmers.

- Blow or suck out the lines feeding the filter or skimmers with a Shop-Vac.

- Plug the return with its stopper.

- Add pool antifreeze to the return lines and skimmer lines if the pool is below ground. Shut down all return and skimmer lines. For above-ground pools, make sure all water has been removed from the lines.

- Drain the water from the filter.

- Check the filtering media and replace it if necessary.

- Disconnect the pump and filter, if possible, and store them. Cover the unit.

- Float large pieces of Styrofoam in pools with liners to reduce the risk of ice damage.

- Cover the pool.

- Remove all pool toys, ladders, and ropes.

- Clean the area around the pool and store any furniture, if you have the room, or pile up chairs and place coverings neatly over them. You can wait until winter to do this.

Repairing a Pool

A pool suffers a bit of wear and tear over time. Between the harsh elements of summer's heat and winter's cold and the erosion of water on paint, tile, and grout, your pool will need to have repairs from time to time. Most people tend to hire their pool repairs out to a professional pool person or have a pool maintenance staff that handles the upkeep of their pool.

Patching Cracks

Hairline cracks in concrete pools can be dealt with by painting the pool with the proper paint, such as epoxy swimming pool paint or chlorinated rubber paint. Larger cracks will need to be patched with an epoxy compound for concrete pools and a fiberglass patch for fiberglass pools (see Figure 19.2). Fiberglass repair kits are sold in pool and spa dealerships, boating equipment stores, and automotive stores.

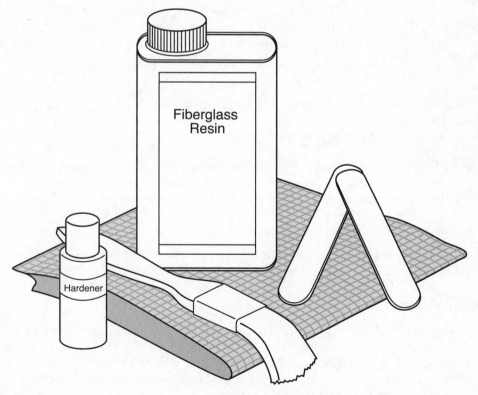

Figure 19.2

Components of a fiberglass kit.

For minor rips in a vinyl pool liner, you can buy a repair kit from a pool dealership. The waterproof bonding agent needs to be applied over the area, and the patch material should be placed on top of it. The repair can be done underwater.

A vinyl liner is less expensive than painting a swimming pool or a fiberglass replacement.

Painting the Pool

Use the same type of paint that exists on the pool to repaint it. There are generally two types of paint: epoxy paint that lasts 5–7 years and chlorinated paint that lasts 2–3 years.

If you have three coats of paint already on your pool, then sandblast the paint off before painting it again. If you're painting on top of paint, make sure the old paint is clean. Clean it with muriatic acid, rinse it, and neutralize it with trisodium phosphate. Rinse it again. Make sure you protect your eyes, skin, and lungs when doing this. Chlorinated rubber paints are self-priming and can be applied directly to the surface. Epoxy paints, however, need a primer—especially over concrete.

I suggest hiring a professional for this job. This is a time-consuming project, and you want to make sure it is done properly with the latest products.

HOT TUBS

After living in Manhattan for over 20 years and experiencing its cold winters, I have become very appreciative of the home that has a hot tub. There is something marvelous about sitting in hot water outside in the freezing cold. Okay, granted I had to drive up to Nyack, New York, to find a friend who had one outside, but it was well worth the trip.

Because hot tubs are mini pools, read the section "Pool Maintenance" first to have a better understanding of checking pH levels, shocking your hot tub, and cleaning it.

Maintenance

The terms *hot tub*, *spa*, and *Jacuzzi* all mean the same thing, although Jacuzzi is a brand name—like Kleenex is to tissues. (The Jacuzzi brothers invented the first whirlpool spa.) Regardless of name, they are all tubs with hot water in them and jets that send out streams of water to make currents and bubbles. Like pools, there are maintenance issues you will need to address with a hot tub.

> **TIP**
>
> For cracks that are larger than 1/8", hire a professional. You want to make sure this job is done properly. A large crack in a concrete pool could mean a structural problem and needs to be dealt with immediately.

> **TIP**
>
> If you are unsure of the type of existing paint on your pool, take a little paint chip into your pool dealership and they will be able to tell you.

Daily:

- Check the sanitizer level.
- Check the pH level.
- Clean the water line with a cleaning paste.

Weekly:

- Shock the spa with a nonchlorine chemical.
- Use a sparkling additive to maintain sparkling water.
- Add a foam control to control foaming.
- If your water is hard, add an antiscaling additive.

Monthly:

- Clean the filter cartridge with a cartridge cleaner.

Yearly:

- Replace the cartridge once a year. This will help your jets to stay powerful.

Troubleshooting

If your tub is not heating, you may want to push the reset button. Next, check to see if your filters are dirty or clogged. If that doesn't work, then you could have a stuck thermostat or a faulty pressure switch or flow switch.

If your tub is getting too hot, then you might have a stuck thermometer or other problems within the system.

Because hot tubs are used year round, you will need to periodically drain the entire tub and refill to keep it clean. *Ozonators* are electric-powered units that help sanitize the water and help reduce the amount of chemicals used.

A quality cover is necessary for a hot tub to keep your utility bill down. Buy a cover that has a core of polystyrene with an R-Value of at least 12 and heat sealed in a marine-grade vinyl that is UV and mildew resistant. Make sure the cover has a reinforced hinge, a zipper, and proper fasteners.

> **Tip**
>
> If you push the reset button and clean the filters and the tub won't heat up or gets overheated, call a professional.

Repairs

Repairing a crack in a hot tub is the same as making a fiberglass repair to a pool. You can pick up kits at a pool equipment, automotive, or boating store. If it is a large crack, seek a professional.

CHECKLIST

❑ Decide on which type of pool's chemicals you have: chlorinated or nonchlorinated.

❑ Check the pH level and balance it with appropriate acid or soda ash.

❑ Shock the pool a few times during the season.

❑ Add algaecide.

❑ Clean your pool often.

❑ Make sure your filter and pump are working properly.

❑ Shut your pool down properly so it is easy to open it up the next season.

❑ Repair small cracks, and hire a professional when needed.

❑ Paint your pool every few years if you have a painted, cement pool.

❑ Follow the same steps for a Jacuzzi or hot tub and use nonchlorinated chemicals.

20

ROOF AND ATTIC

The attic and the roof were a bit scary and were off-limits to me as a child. Our attic was the place we kept suitcases, old Halloween costumes, and Christmas decorations. I was fascinated by it since it required pulling down a string to reveal the staircase. Once the stairs were unfolded, I could gingerly walk up and pull another string to turn on a light to see the stored treasures of the season. What intrigued me was the possibility of seeing a flying squirrel in a trap. It was an awful finding because I loved all creatures and, heck, these squirrels could fly for goodness sake. Didn't that make them worthy of not being trapped?

The roof was too dangerous for me to get on it. Not only did it have a decent slope, but there was also quite a drop off the back of the house. Now, years later, whenever I work on a roof, I am extremely careful and like to work as safely as possible. I think the hardest part of roof work is getting onto the roof from the ladder. Once you master that, you're home free. I suggest that everyone work within his or her comfort level. If you are the least bit uneasy about getting on your roof, hire the work out to the professionals.

The attic and roof are tied together because a well-insulated and ventilated attic directly affects the longevity of the roof's materials above it. First, let's take a look at the structure of the roof.

Roof

There are two types of roofs: pitched (also called sloped) and flat. Most homes have a pitched roof, whereas commercial buildings and apartments have flat roofs. The location of your home influences the slope of your roof. In areas that receive heavy snowfall, a decent pitch to the roof is needed since you wouldn't want a buildup of snow and ice on a flat roof. You will find more flat roofs in mild and arid climates.

The slope is known as the *pitch* of the roof (see Figure 20.1). You may hear a roof described as a 4-to-12 pitch or slope. This means that if you held a level against the roof, for every horizontal 12" (run), there would be a 4" drop (rise).

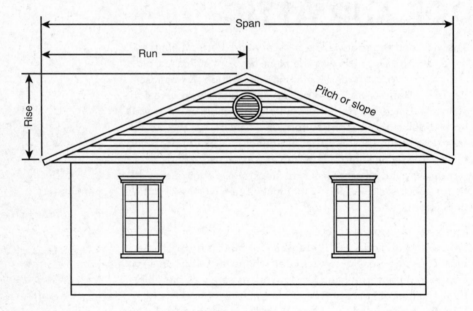

FIGURE 20.1

The pitch of a roof is determined by the rise and the run.

Many components make up your roof, as described in the following sections.

Rafters or Trusses

Rafters or trusses are the frame that gives the roof its shape and support. A contractor has two choices when building a roof: cutting and assembling a complex roof system from scratch, known as *rafters*, or ordering *trusses* that are prefabricated in factories. Rafters that are cut by hand and are open allow you to have an attic space because they are tied into the ridge beam and then angled to lie on the top plate (see

Figure 20.2). Trusses are prebuilt structural members designed to carry the load of the roof to the outside walls of the home (see Figure 20.3). These are brought to the job site where they are lifted in place by a crane or manually lifted with the help of two people and then are attached. This type of roof system has become quite popular because it allows builders to work quickly without compromising the roof's integrity.

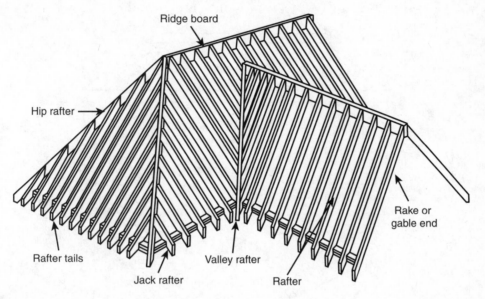

FIGURE 20.2

Some common roof terms are rafter, ridge, hip, and valley.

Roofers use a roofing square to determine the correct angle to cut the rafters. When I was in carpenter's school, we learned to make a birds mouth in the rafter that sits on the cap plate (see Figure 20.4). This was how all rafters sat on the top plate. This method has been replaced with metal rafter ties. The overhang of rafter or truss creates the soffit around the house.

Sheathing

Once the frame of the roof is in place, the covering (made of plywood, wafer-board, or particleboard) is nailed to the frame. If your home has wood shakes, you will probably have sheathing of 1×4 wood slats to prevent the wood shakes from rotting. The most common sheathing is C/D grade (it has a lower grade and cost) plywood, particleboard, or wafer-board. The thickness will vary from 3/8" to 3/4" depending on local building codes.

Once the sheathing has been laid, a drip edge is installed around the perimeter of the roofline, known as the eaves.

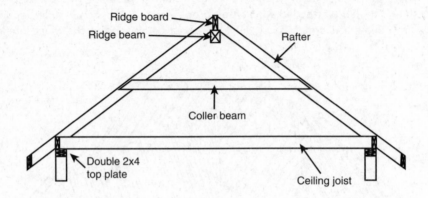

Rafter roof system

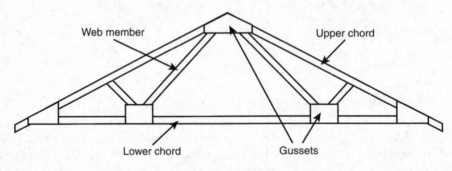

Truss roof system

FIGURE 20.3

A truss roof system ties into the ridge beam and to the top plate.

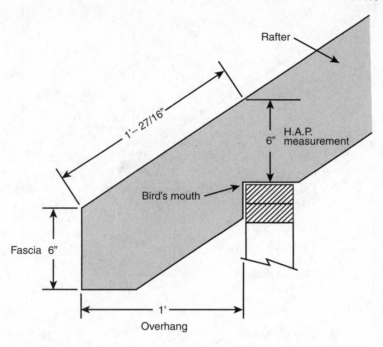

FIGURE 20.4

A birds mouth *is a notch cut into a rafter to enable it to sit on the top plate.*

Roof Covering

After the sheathing has been fastened to the roof's frame and the drip edge is in place, the *underlayment* and roof covering is then installed to protect the sheathing from the weather. The *underlayment* is the thin material used on top of the sheathing and is necessary to keep moisture out of the house. The most popular underlayment is roofing felt, an asphalt-saturated felt resistant to the elements. Synthetic underlayment is made of synthetic polymers and is usually more durable than asphalt-saturated felt. Underlayment is laid lengthwise across the entire roof starting at the bottom and continuing up. Each strip is fastened to the sheathing by nails or staples and overlaps the strip below it. The second coat of felt is attached to the bottom layer with adhesive and overlaps the strip below it, ensuring that the joints don't fall in the same place as the paper underneath it. Figure 20.5 shows a roof's sheathing, felt, and tile.

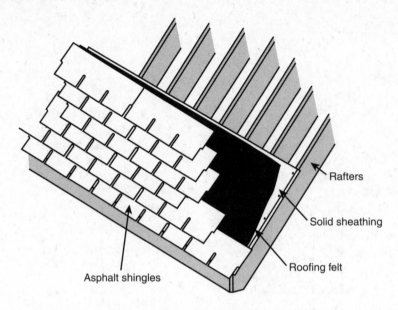

Rafters

Solid sheathing

Roofing felt

Asphalt shingles

FIGURE 20.5

Components of a roof: layers of sheathing, roofing felt, and tile.

The most common problems occur from laying the felt paper on sheathing that is not completely dry, not overlapping each strip, and not applying it smoothly.

Other applications can help prolong the life of your roof, such as a waterproof coating and solar paint. A waterproof coating or membrane can be applied to the roof felt or on top of asphalt shingles, depending on your need. These membranes are flexible and provide a great solution to a leaky roof, and using a waterproof membrane is necessary on flat roofs. Solar paint can be used to reflect the heat off a roof that receives an abundance of sun exposure. This is mostly used on metal roofs to bring the temperature down in the living space or attic below.

Most residential roofs are covered with shingles, but there are many other types of coverings as well, including tile, slate, and metal.

There are two types of roof shingles: organic and glass fiber. *Organic shingles* are made of organic felt paper saturated with asphalt to make them waterproof. *Glass fiber shingles* use a glass fiber reinforcing paper or mat in the shape of a shingle. The paper is then coated with asphalt to make it waterproof. The organic asphalt shingle contains 40% more asphalt in 100 square feet than the glass fiber shingle, giving it more blow-off resistance.

If your roof has asphalt shingles, make sure there is a starter strip, which becomes the backing for the first visible row of shingles. This starter strip helps to prevent water from getting underneath the shingles at the notches and between the tabs. Shingles are laid starting at the bottom of the roof and are then lapped and staggered so the joint of the shingle below one shingle does not align with the joint of the shingle on top of it.

Clay tiles are an excellent choice of roofing material if you live in a warmer climate. A clay tile roof is most often associated with Spanish-style homes. There are three grades of clay tile, the first being the most resistant to severe frost and the third having relatively no resistance. Because clay tile can last for many years and is relatively maintenance free, it is recommended you install a high-performance underlayment. You may also need to install additional roof supports to hold the weight of the tiles.

Most clay tiles are installed using mortar and nails, although builders in Florida have been using adhesives that seem to outperform mortar in hurricane-force winds.

Wood shakes are made of cedar and are split by hand or resawn. A resawn shake has one side that looks irregular and one side that is cut thinner to give the shingle a tapered look. Hand-split shakes are tapered with a more natural look.

Slate is one of the oldest roofing materials found in the United States and is mainly used in the northeast. Slate is split into thin slabs and is extremely durable. Much like a clay tile roof, the roof needs to be able to handle the weight and may need added supports. This is a job for a professional, and finding professionals who know how to properly install a slate roof can be challenging.

Metal shingles interlock and are made of aluminum, stainless steel, or copper. These are lightweight roofing materials that will not crack, rot, split, or burn and can last 50 years or more.

Flashing

Usually the last defense from water penetration is *roof flashing*. Flashing blocks water from getting into joints and underneath the roof covering through natural conditions such as wind, gravity, and surface tension. Flashing comes in the form of a flexible membrane known as an *ice guard* or in sheet metal. The most typical types of sheet metal are aluminum, copper, lead-coated copper, galvanized steel, stainless steel, lead, and zinc. The flexible sheet metal is installed in the valley of the roof and around the roof's vents, chimneys, skylights, eaves, rakes, ridges, and the intersections of the roof to the wall.

A drip edge is the first piece of flashing you will need to install before laying the felt paper. The drip edge runs along the edge of the eaves or the perimeter of the roofline. Once the drip edge is in place, the felt paper is rolled out and secured. Flashing is then laid down on the ridges and in the valleys before the shingles are put on. Around vents and chimneys, the flashing is on top of the shingles below it and then overlapped with the shingles above it.

Depending on how severe your weather is, you might need an ice guard membrane on your roof and its valleys.

Drainage

A major design consideration for all roofs is drainage, which removes water from the roof. If you have a large enough overhang on your roof and the water is quickly absorbed into the ground and routed away from your home, you may not need a gutter system. For everyone else, installing gutters will save you money in repairs in the future since water can be the most damaging element to your home.

Gutters and downspouts are made from vinyl, aluminum, galvanized steel, stainless steel, and copper, and you can buy sectional or seamless gutters. Sectional types are sold with matching corners, end caps, downspouts, and other fittings and can be purchased at your neighborhood home center. Seamless gutters are brought to your home by a gutter fabricator. They are formed without joints and come in one long piece. The lengths join to outside and inside corner components and downspout outlets.

The gutter system is attached to the eaves by various straps, brackets, and hangers (see Figure 20.6). Always seal the joints with silicone caulk, and use leaf protectors that snap in place or lay over the gutter to prevent debris from falling in and obstructing the flow of water.

Clean your gutters once every few months and more often in the fall and spring.

Gutters are composed of the gutters and downspouts.

Moss, Lichens, Mold, and Algae

We live in a world with live spores floating around us at all times. Moss, lichens, mold, and algae can easily grow on your roof given the right conditions: shade and moisture. Once these spores take root, they can grab underneath your roofing material and create a channel for water to get into your home. You can spot mold on your roof because it makes dark, blackened patches.

TIP

Always install hurricane straps or clips in areas where hurricanes and high winds are a problem (see Figure 20.7). These straps are stronger than the common practice of toenailing the rafters and trusses to the walls. These clips or straps hold the roof in place in case of high winds.

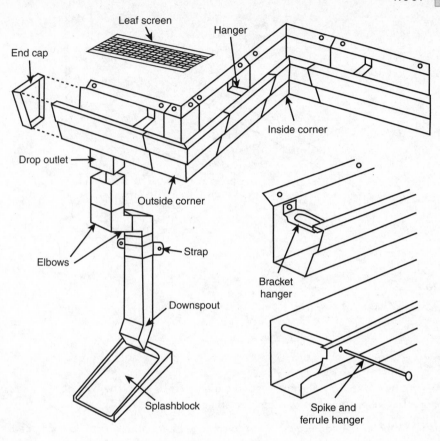

FIGURE 20.6

The components of a gutter.

There are various products you can use to wash your roof and remove such growth. Never use a high-power washer, though—instead, use a low-power washer to apply the solution. This will keep your roofing material in tact.

You can also install zinc strips against the ridge cap on both sides of the peak to inhibit fungus, moss, and algae. When it rains, the water time releases the zinc carbonate, which is a fungistat, and it runs down the roof preventing fungus, algae, and moss growth.

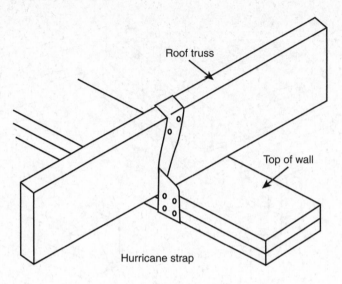

FIGURE 20.7

Hurricane straps hold the roof to the walls in case of high winds.

ATTIC

The attic needs to be well ventilated and insulated to keep the roof above it in good shape, the living space below it comfortable, and the utility bill low.

The air in the attic needs to circulate to remove heat and moisture that can cause damp rot and mold. Moisture and heat buildup can cause the sheathing and rafters to rot, the shingles to buckle, and the insulation to break down.

There are various ways to move this hot, moist air. One is to use vents that keep the air moving through the attic. If you have an overhang created by the bottom of the roof, install soffit vents. These help draw air from the bottom of the attic up to the top. The best scenario is to use a continuous ridge vent at the peak of the roof. This type of vent is installed when a house is built or when the roof needs to be replaced. Gable vents are great to have underneath the peak of the roof to allow air to flow out at the ends. Roof vents are installed on the top of the roof and usually come with a fan to help remove stale air. Turbines also sit on top of the roof and use the air pressure along with the wind to push the vanes of the turbine and make it spin.

Insulation is also very important in the attic between the joists of the ceiling below. Always install the correct R-Value insulation for your area. Use baffles between the rafters of the roof to keep that air flowing up from the soffit. This way, the insulation can be up against the baffles and you won't worry that you have covered the soffit vents.

Those of you who would like to finish your attic into a living space will need to install insulation between the rafters and then finish the pitched ceiling and walls with drywall or paneling.

For more information about ventilation, insulation, and R-values, refer to Chapter 15, "Insulation and Ventilation."

CHECKLIST

❑ Install proper underlayment and drip edge to your roof's sheathing.

❑ Use an ice guard membrane if you live in a cold climate.

❑ Make sure you flash around all vent stacks, chimneys, and vents.

❑ Install gutters to properly divert water away from your home.

❑ Clean the gutters so they do not become clogged.

❑ Install zinc strips to remove fungus, algae, and moss from your roof.

❑ Ventilate your attic to remove the heat and moisture.

❑ Insulate your attic with the proper R-Value.

Security Systems

Feeling safe in your home is non-negotiable criteria for living on this planet! Everyone wants to feel safe in the confines of their home, and with the security and alarm systems available, there's no reason you shouldn't.

Security System Design

The design of a security system depends on the needs of the inhabitants of the home and your budget. Some security systems offer more of an alarm-type security and detect if there is an intrusion in a door or window or movement in a room. More advanced systems have surveillance features that let you monitor and observe the environmental conditions inside and outside your home with cameras and sensors. Some systems allow you to observe this from a computer away from the home or through a telephone. Obviously, the more bells and whistles you want, the more money you'll spend. For this reason, it is important to know your options to secure the inside and outside of your home.

The design of a security system should protect the entire perimeter of the house. Some systems detect window and door intrusion, sound, motion, body heat, and air movement. When designing your security system, you will want to keep in mind the lifestyle of your family and the location of items that need to be protected, such as jewelry, art, and collectibles. Always make sure you have enough smoke and fire alerting sensors, and discuss with your family the best emergency response.

If you hire a security company to install your security system, they will go through your home and give you their suggestions

IN THIS CHAPTER

- Designing a security system to fit your needs
- Understanding the difference between wireless and hard-wired systems
- Fire detection and environmental sensors

on locations of movement or heat sensors, smoke detectors, cameras, keypads, and so on. They will also install the system for you. Those who buy a wireless system and plan to install it themselves will need to figure out the best location of the sensors and detectors in your home. First, you must think like a criminal and look at your home through his eyes. How would a person get in? Do the following:

- **Draw a rough blueprint of your home, unless you have an actual blueprint**—Use this to help you configure your system and keep track of what you will need.

- **Count the number of windows and doors in your home**—You will need to buy a sensor for each window and door.

- **Consider the placement of motion detectors**—Motion detectors should be placed in the corner of a room with the best view of the entire room and its entrance. Be sure to think this through. Those of you who like to get up in the middle of the night might not want a motion detector installed in areas of the home that you use in the middle of the night. Consider your pets roaming around the house, too. This is why every system can vary slightly with each household. Some people like to have motion detectors on only in the basement when they sleep.

- **Count your bedrooms and living spaces**—Include the kitchen and basement to give you the number of smoke detectors you'll need. Carbon monoxide detectors should be located near sleeping areas and on every level of the home. For extra protection, install one in every bedroom.

Wireless Systems

If you want to save money, you can buy security systems and set them up yourself. Wireless security systems are popular because you don't have to fool with running wires through your wall or tacking them at the bottom of the baseboards and because they can be purchased at your local hardware store. They use battery-powered radio transmitters and receivers that connect the system's sensors, smoke and fire detectors, sirens, cameras, video displays, and keypads.

The upside to these systems is that they are easy to install, don't require hiding wires, and can be placed in areas that are too hard to hardwire. You can also bring these systems with you when you move. The downside to wireless security systems is that they require periodic battery replacement. If you forget to replace the batteries, then that component is useless. You are also susceptible to electromagnetic interference in some locations. Electromagnetic interference is emitted by electrical circuits and the interconnection of electrical elements such as transistors, resistors, inductors, and so on. In our high-tech world we have to live around such interference, which affects the reception of AM and FM radio and television reception without cable or satellite. The radio range of a wireless system has a limit to distance. Obviously, if you build your home, you can install a hard-wired system during the build.

Hard-wired Systems

A hard-wired system uses AC power as the primary source of power and has a battery backup in case of power outages. It has the same monitoring capabilities as a wireless system, such as sensors, smoke and fire detectors, sirens, cameras, video displays, and keypads. A hard-wired system is more reliable than a wireless system because it is not affected by distance or interference due to it not using a radio frequency to communicate with the system. Other advantages are that a hard-wired system doesn't require batteries (except for the system's backup), which allows the components to be smaller and allows cameras and some motion sensors to be hidden in the wall (all that's required is a small hole to allow it to do its job). These systems are often installed at the beginning of a home's construction, making them an integral part of the home and more pleasing to the eye.

The downside is that a hard-wired system must be installed by professionals, making it more expensive. Plus, you usually lease it from a security company. Because this system is wired into the home's electricity, it becomes an integral part of the home and you cannot take it with you if you move. For areas where you cannot wire through the wall, such as a stonewall, the component has an exposed wire, jeopardizing the system's integrity if someone were to cut the wire.

Hard-wired security systems are often connected to the phone line and monitored by an emergency response center. If the alarm goes off, the emergency response center calls the house to see if an alarm went off by accident before they alert the police or fire department. You can usually reset the system with your keypad, which is the brain center to the security system. If the alarm goes off by accident, the emergency response center calls you and you need to give them your password to identify yourself.

SAFETY CONCERNS

When we think of a security system, we usually think of how we can protect our homes from burglars and riffraff; however, there are other concerns we need to keep in mind, such as fire and environmental concerns. Even though most homeowners will not need environmental detectors to help with their crops, it is still a good idea to detect the climate outside if you have a summer home and want to keep an eye on the property's needs, such as calling someone to bleed the pipes when it gets too cold.

Heat Sensors, Smoke Detectors, and Carbon Monoxide Detectors

Fire detection is handled in two different ways. One is a heat sensor that monitors a rapid rise in temperature. When the heat gets to a fixed temperature, the alarm sounds and the security company is notified. Heat sensors are part of a hard-wired system. The other sensor for fire detection is a smoke detector. This monitors only smoke. Some people have both heat and smoke detectors. But if you have to choose, go with a smoke detector. They should be placed in your sleeping areas, mounted on the ceiling or 6"-12" below the ceiling; in living spaces such as basements, kitchens, and family rooms; and on every level of the home. Smoke detectors come in hard-wired systems and wireless systems. If you buy a battery-operated smoke detector, change the batteries twice a year. I like to change the batteries the two times a year I have to set my clock backward and forward for daylight savings time to help me better remember.

Carbon monoxide is a poisonous, odorless gas that is produced whenever fuel is burned. Household appliances such as ovens, ranges, clothes dryers, and oil or gas furnaces give off carbon monoxide. These appliances usually will not cause a problem if they are properly vented. Fireplaces, charcoal grills, and a running car also produce carbon monoxide.

Carbon monoxide detectors sound a warning before poisonous carbon monoxide levels reach 100 parts per million over 90 minutes. These detectors are important to install on the ceiling at least near sleeping areas of the home and on every level. Do not install these near a fuel-burning appliance, within 15' of cooking or heating appliances, or in humid rooms such as a bathroom.

If your detector goes off, open all the windows immediately to vent out your space and make sure you call a professional technician to fix the problem on your appliance. If members in your home are experiencing dizziness, headaches, or vomiting, call 911 and/or the fire department immediately and move to fresh air.

Environmental Sensors

Those who live in rural areas on a vineyard, a farm, an orchard, or a ranch might want to have environmental sensors. Environmental sensors can detect humidity, temperature, and barometric pressure. Temperature sensors come in handy when monitoring a vacation home, water pipes, a furnace, computer rooms, or other areas of the house that could be damaged by extreme temperatures.

CHECKLIST

❑ Make a list of entrance points in your home.

❑ Decide on lighting, motion detectors, and alarms in relation to the living habits of your family.

❑ Decide if an emergency response center works for your family in case of burglary or fire.

❑ Choose the right environmental sensors to fit your landscape and home.

SEPTIC SYSTEMS

Years ago I visited the Chateau de Versailles. While others marveled over the beautiful detailed work, landscape, and fountains, I was obsessed with one piece of information the guide had told us. The castle had been built without a sanitation system in mind; therefore, there were palace lackeys who toted around portable toilet chairs. Their job was to bring the toilet to the person in need and then dispose of it.

I've had some bad jobs in my life, but that one would take the cake! The thought of a sloshing toilet chair being carried around that beautiful palace has never left my mind! Eccckkk!

I constantly feel blessed being born in the twentieth century. Running water and a toilet are really luxuries. When we brush our teeth, wash dishes, or use the toilet, the water we use goes out to a septic system. Most of us take it all for granted until something goes haywire, and then we have to deal with a clogged toilet or a backed-up septic system filling our bathtub—which recently happened to me. (Turns out that the clay sewage pipes that run from my house to the county's sewage system are cracked. The tree roots got into the cracks and caused a huge blockage in the line. Every 6–8 months now a plumber has to come out and take a large, motorized auger or snake to cut through the roots.)

There are a couple of ways sewage is handled: either privately in your backyard by a septic tank or by an urban waste water system that sends the waste through underground pipes to a city-owned facility.

22

IN THIS CHAPTER

- Understanding the type of sewer system your home uses: urban waste water system or a septic tank
- Types of septic drain systems
- Maintaining your septic system
- Troubleshooting your septic system

URBAN WASTE WATER SYSTEMS

If you live in an urban area, most likely you have a septic system that takes the sewage to a waste water treatment facility. These sewer systems use gravity to make the waste water flow downhill to the facility, which is usually in a low-lying area. In case of a hill, lift stations and grinder pumps move the sewage up and over high areas.

Most sewer pipes are 3'-5' in diameter and are usually located in the middle of the street. The pipe leading from your house to the main sewer pipe is at a slope, allowing the waste water to drain into the large city-owned waste pipes. Manhole covers offer a way in to the sewer system in case your area has a problem.

Water at the waste water treatment facility usually goes through a few stages of treatment depending on how sophisticated the system is and how much money your county has. The first stage is the primary treatment, which is similar to a septic tank. (I discuss septic tanks in the following section.) The waste water goes through a screen and then dumps into a series of pools or ponds that let the water stand, allowing the scum to rise and the solids to settle down. The solids are then collected and disposed of in an incinerator or a landfill.

The primary treatment removes most of the solids, bacteria, and organic materials. If the treatment facility only has a primary treatment, the water is treated with chlorine to kill the bacteria and discharged back into the environment.

The secondary treatment uses a large tank filled with bacteria to eat through nutrients and organic materials. Then the water is sent to large tanks where the bacteria settles out.

The third stage is the tertiary treatment, which involves the use of chemicals to remove nitrogen and phosphorus; sometimes filter beds are used, too. To kill any remaining bacteria, chlorine is added in a large chlorination tank before the water is discharged.

If you have a problem in your drain line, you will need to call a professional to come to your home and clear the pipes inside the home. If that doesn't fix the problem, he will investigate further by checking the drain's clean-out opening located just outside the home or in the basement or crawlspace. The cap to the clean-out usually has a square fitting that can be removed with an open-ended wrench. This opening will allow the plumber to clear the drain line with a power auger between your home and the city's sewer pipe.

SEPTIC TANKS

Those who live outside the city have septic tanks. The septic tank does everything a waste water facility does, just on a smaller scale.

A septic tank is a huge, box-like tank made of concrete or steel that is buried in your yard, usually in the back. The waste water from your home flows into the tank at one end through a solid pipe that deposits the waste toward the bottom of the tank. The solid materials drop to the bottom, creating the sludge layer. All the materials that float rise to the top, forming the scum layer. In the middle of the two lies water (see Figure 22.1).

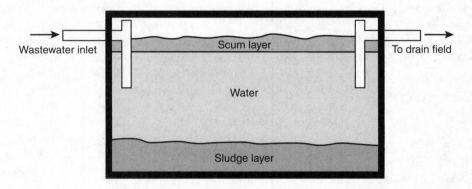

FIGURE 22.1

Components of a septic tank.

The bacteria in the waste water breaks down the organic material, creating gases that smell like...well, they don't smell very good. This is why your home has P-traps underneath the sink and in the toilet. The P-trap traps water in the bend, creating a seal between the top of your drain and the septic tank so you don't smell the gas. This is one of the reasons your home's plumbing has vents, which are the pipes that lead out through the top of the roof. These gases need some place to escape and it's best to escape over your home than in it!

The bacteria that breaks down the solid organic matter comes from your digestive system, so you do not need to add anything to your septic system, although with many cleaning detergents containing hydrocarbons, phenols, and sulfur, the bacteria can break down. You can buy a flushable product in powder or liquid form that flushes down your toilet and restores the bacteria. Do this once a month to keep a balanced toilet system.

The septic tank needs to be pumped every 2–5 years, depending on use, to remove excess scum or sludge, which can eventually clog the drain field lines. There should be an inspection pipe and a manhole cover to access the septic tank. Always hire a professional to pump the tank through the manhole cover, not the inspection pipes. Make sure it is cleaned completely and have the tank checked for leaks. You can find a specialist under "Septic Tanks" in the phone book.

Chapter 22	Septic Systems

To determine where your septic tank is located, notice where your drain pipe leaves the house and look in that direction. In winter, the tank is usually the first place snow melts and the last place frost forms. If you cannot find your septic tank, go to your local health department to see if they have your building records. Once you find the manhole cover, make sure you mark it for further use.

Trench Drain Field

Most septic systems have a trench system for a drain field. When new water enters the septic tank, it pushes out the water that has been sitting in the tank (between the sludge and scum layer) through a solid pipe and into a distribution box. Several perforated pipes are attached to the distribution box, and they route the waste water into a drain field. The trenches that hold the perforated pipes are usually about 4'-6' deep and approximately 2' wide. The gravel fills about half the depth of the trenches, and the perforated pipes (usually about 4" in diameter) sit on top of the gravel and are then covered with dirt.

The dissolved wastes and bacteria in the waste water are either absorbed into the soil particles or decomposed naturally by micro-organisms. This process is necessary to remove any disease-causing organisms. The waste water is then purified and either evaporates or goes back into the ground water (see Figure 22.2).

The ground's absorption determines the size of the drain field. If your ground is hard clay, your drain field will have to take up a good bit of space.

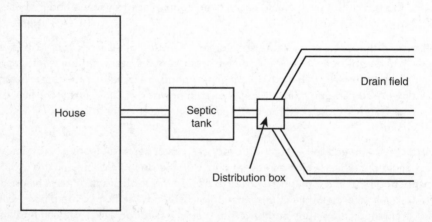

FIGURE 22.2

Drain field pipes distribute sewage into the ground where it breaks down and is absorbed.

Seepage Pit or Dry Well

An alternative to the trench system is the seepage pit or dry well (see Figure 22.3). There is no distribution box in this setup. Instead, a solid pipe leads from the house to the septic tank, and then a solid pipe leads to a precast tank with holes on the sides. This tank is dug down into the soil and surrounded by gravel. Older systems have a tank made of brick or stone without mortar to allow the waste water to flow out between the joints.

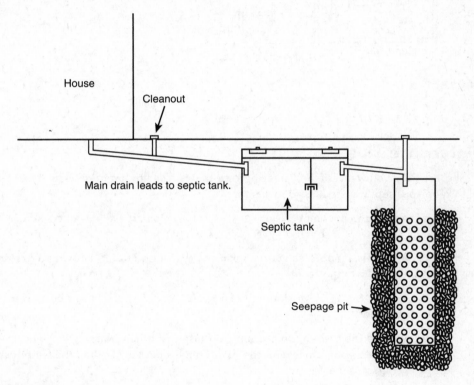

FIGURE 22.3

A sewage pit.

Sand Mound System

If your house is in an area with too much clay and the water cannot properly absorb into the ground, you might need to use a sand mound system (see Figure 22.4). This system has a typical septic tank, but it also has a solid pipe leading to a pumping chamber. The pumping chamber pumps the waste water to perforated pipes that lay under a mound of sand that has been put on top of the soil. This mound of sand is large and deep enough to handle the treatment of the waste water, which is used to evaporate or be used to feed vegetation growing on top of it.

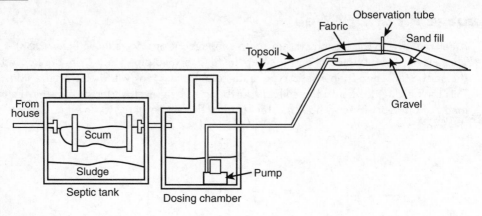

FIGURE 22.4

A sand mound system.

Maintenance Tips

The last thing you want is a foul-smelling yard that is a health hazard. Follow these tips to keep your septic system in good shape:

- Have the septic tank pumped every 2–5 years to remove the sludge and scum buildup, and have it inspected every 3 years.

- Put paper towels, diapers, sanitary napkins, tampons, and other hardy material in the trash and not down the toilet.

- Never pour oils or fats down your kitchen drain. They can solidify and clog up the septic tank pipes.

- Never overload the system. Do not run your dishwasher and washing machine at peak hours when your family uses the bathroom for bathing. Spread the water usage over the course of the day.

- Always fix any leaks and install low-flow fixtures to cut down on water use.

- Instead of using a garbage disposal, set up a compost system outside. Garbage disposals can overload a septic system with too many solids.

- Never dump caustic liquids, such as solvents, paint thinner, cleaning fluid, and pesticides, down the drain.

- Never drive vehicles over the septic system.

- Do not plant trees or shrubs over the tank or drain field. The roots can clog or damage the system.

Troubleshooting

Wet or standing water can occur over the drain field for the following reasons:

- The tank has not been pumped out in the past 5 years and has clogged pipes.
- The drain field pipes are clogged by tree roots.
- The pipes are broken and not properly dispersing the waste water.
- The homeowners use too much water, and the septic system cannot handle the amount used. Spread out the times of showering, washing dishes, and doing laundry.

The following can cause toilets to back up or run slowly or bathtubs and basements to flood with sewage:

- A plugged drain line leading to the septic system or sewer system
- A plugged pipe in the inlet or outlet pipe to the septic tank
- A backed-up drain field or a clog in the drain field pipes
- A septic tank that needs to be pumped

TIP

Keep the runoff of rainwater from your roof and downspouts directed away from the drain field to avoid excess saturation.

CHECKLIST

- ❑ Have your septic tank pumped every 2-5 years depending on use, and have it inspected every 3 years.
- ❑ Be mindful of the solids you put down your waste system. Throw larger paper items and tampons in the trash.
- ❑ Redirect your rainwater so it doesn't puddle over the drain field.
- ❑ Stretch out your home's water use throughout the day so you do not overload the septic system.

Staircases

I grew up in a ranch home. Fortunately, we had a basement that gave us a staircase, but it wasn't the kind of staircase I had fancied myself to have. Maybe it was the *Brady Bunch* family's staircase or the one in *Gone With the Wind*. It could have been the old photos of my mom in her beautiful wedding dress at the bottom of a sexy, curved staircase, but I was certainly supposed to have grown up in a home with a long, flowing staircase that I could have ridden down the banister to meet my friends at the door.

Being an optimist, I tried to look on the bright side. At least I didn't have to worry about the squeaky stairs waking up my parents when I snuck out of the house!

Staircase Components

If you have stairs in your home, you know that not only do the stairs add a nice touch to your home, but over time they can have some repairs that need to be attended to.

First, you need to know the components that make up a staircase (see Figure 23.1).

- **Handrail**—Also known as the *banister*. The handrail is an important feature to the safety of a person going up and down the staircase. It is most important that the handrail is firmly supported by the spindles and newel posts or is attached to the wall.

- **Newel posts**—The sturdy posts located at the top, bottom, and landing of the staircase that support the handrail.

Chapter 23 | Staircases

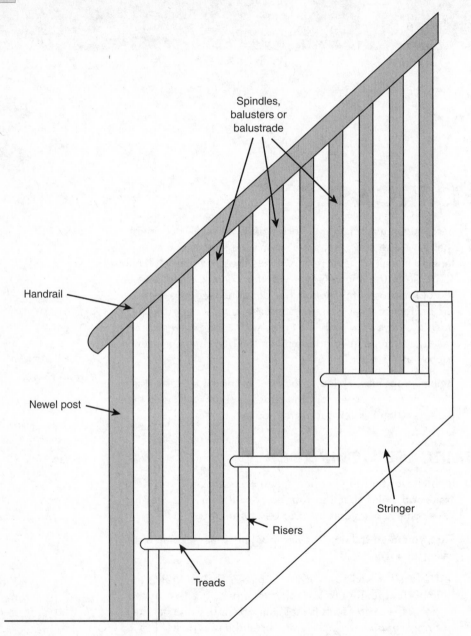

Spindles, balusters or balustrade

Handrail

Newel post

Risers

Stringer

Treads

FIGURE 23.1

Parts of a staircase.

- **Spindles**—The same thing as balusters and balustrades. They are the slender, vertical supports in a staircase that hold up the handrail. These vertical supports are usually referred to as *spindles* when they're installed in a hole in the tread itself. There are usually two or three spindles in each tread.

- **Treads**—These are what you step on. They are usually *bull-nosed*, which means the edge of the tread is rounded over.

- **Risers**—The vertical part of each step. Some staircases do not have risers to give them a more open feeling.

- **Stringers**—These support the stair treads and risers together. They are underneath the treads and are either open or closed. An *open* riser means the stringer is notched out for the treads to fit in. A *closed* stringer has the treads routed into the sides of the stringer.

The Rise and the Run

You will hear the terms *rise* and *run* of a staircase. The rise is the distance between the top of a stair and the top of the stair above it. This measurement will be consistent throughout the staircase. The run refers to the depth of the tread. On most staircases the rise is around 7" or 7 1/2", with the tread around 11".

The *total rise* is the distance between the bottom landing and the top landing. The *total run* is the horizontal distance of the run units.

Common Problems

The most common problems that occur in a staircase are the treads coming loose, which causes squeaking, and the spindles or balusters coming loose. If you can get underneath the staircase, fixing the treads is easy. You will need to attach an L bracket from the underside of the tread to the stringer. If you cannot get underneath the staircase, you will have to make the repair from above. Squeaky stair kits are available that allow you to make this fix even through carpet, if you have that on your stairs. Otherwise, you can secure the tread to the stringer with a trim screw that has a smaller head.

The balusters or spindles can become loose and require glue and a finish nail toe-nailed through the bottom of the baluster into the tread at an angle.

It is important to have a stable handrail. An intricate handrail will have a *gooseneck*, which is what the handrail looks like when it goes down to a landing or around a corner. If the fix is over your head, make sure you hire a professional. Make sure your handrail is sturdy and stable—you never know when someone may want to glide down the banister!

ATTIC STAIRS

If you have an attic, then you should definitely have attic stairs for easy access (see Figure 23.2). Make sure you frame out the opening according to the manufacturer's specifications. It's also good to have a light in the attic with the switch near attic the opening.

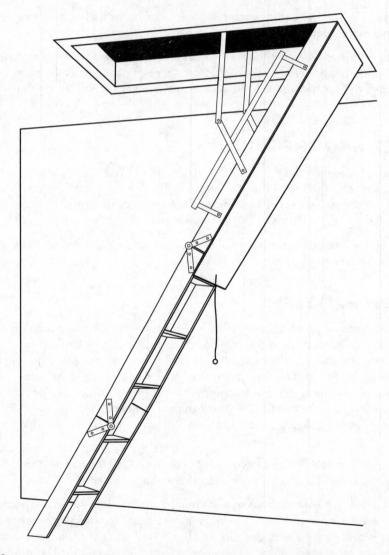

FIGURE 23.2

A folding attic staircase.

As with any stairs, always make sure the treads are in sound condition. If you need to replace a tread, then remove it and use it as a template to make your new tread. If your stairs are old and feeling unsafe, you can remove the folding stairs and replace them.

CHECKLIST

❑ Make sure all your staircase components are structurally sound.

❑ Repair or replace any treads, spindles, or handrails if they're not properly secure.

❑ Make sure all the treads on foldable attic stairs are secure and can hold your weight.

❑ Replace any attic treads when necessary, or replace the entire staircase when needed.

TELEPHONE SYSTEMS AND COMPUTERS

My family was not the household that answers the phone huffing and puffing. That's because I grew up in a three-bedroom ranch house that had seven phones in it. You see, my dad worked for the telephone company and sold phone systems, so every room in the house had a phone.

Those of you who are old enough will remember dial phones. It was quite a leap to remember a phone number when phones changed to a touchtone keypad since the pattern was much different from a rotary dial. Of course, now I haven't a clue as to what anyone's number is because I have voice-activated calling on my cell phone and can add people's names to my home phone directory with the touch of a button.

I will share with you one neat little trick that I learned after watching a series of old movies when a desperate character would frantically press the receiver to get the operator. Did you know that works? Yes, it does. If you have a corded phone with a receiver button (hang-up button) and press the receiver button quickly 10 times, it becomes an O for the operator even if you have a touchtone phone. Similarly, you can dial any number you want by quickly tapping the numbers out with a slight pause between them. Don't believe me? Try it!

TYPES OF PHONE SYSTEMS

There are various types of phone systems available. Most people have touchtone phones for the convenience of handling those annoying automated voicemail systems—and let's face it, the rotary dial is antiquated. Similarly, many people have

24

Chapter 24 Telephone Systems and Computers

TIP

Keep a corded phone in case of a power outage. A cordless phone works if you have electricity, but if the power goes dead, you will not have a working phone system. Fortunately, when the blackout occurred in Manhattan, I had corded phones to use to call people. If you're thinking that it doesn't matter since you have a cell phone, don't forget that cell phones need to be recharged by an electrical outlet or through your car adapter.

NOTE

Bring the old battery with you to the electronics store when replacing it. You'll see that there are close to a bazillion types of batteries for cordless phones, and it can get confusing if you don't have your battery with you. Some electronic stores will take your old battery and recycle it.

replaced corded phones with cordless phones. No matter what type of phone you have, they all get the job done.

There are two ways to send a signal: analog or digital. *Analog* lines are referred to as *Plain Old Telephone System (POTS)*. These lines are found in your home or a small office building and transfer audio or video signals through electronic pulses. In large office buildings, a *digital* signal is used to transmit audio and video in a binary format of 1s and 0s. You can tell whether your phone is an analog phone by looking at the back of it. If it says it complies with part 68, FCC Rules, and REN (ringer equivalence number), the phone line is analog. A digital phone line usually needs to have the number 9 dialed for an outside line or has multiple function keys on the dial pad.

When you buy a cordless phone, you will notice that they are either analog or digital, which specifies the signal from the base to the receiver; they all connect to the outside analog line using an analog device, however. An analog cordless phone often has a good bit of interference, and your neighbor can possibly tune in to your phone call if he has a similar phone system and is close enough. This is why 900MHz phones have been replaced with 2.8GHz phones. The latest models are 5.8GHz and come in digital format. These are powerful, clear, and secure and do not interfere with wireless Internet connections.

The Phone Line

Most phone companies are responsible for the wiring to your home. Once it enters the home, though, any problems are up to you to repair. If you have the phone company make the repair, you will be charged a stiff fee for an easy job that, in most cases, you can handle yourself. Phone cords, jacks, and telephone wire are inexpensive and easy to replace. If your wireless phone is dead, you may need to replace the battery. Wireless phone batteries have lasted me up to 4 years or more.

You can add more jacks to your home by attaching the color wires of an extension phone wire to the matching color terminals that are marked R, G, Y, and B and running the wire to another part of your home. You will then attach another jack to the end of these wires. You usually will only need to attach the R and G wires.

The Internet

There was a time not too long ago when the only way to connect to the Internet was through a dial-up service through your phone line. Now there are five ways: analog, Integrated Services Digital Network (ISDN), Digital Subscriber Line (DSL), cable, and satellite. If you want to have an Internet connection in your home, you will want to get familiar with these terms.

Analog

An analog connection is the original way most of us had to log on to the Internet. All you need is a phone line for this type of connection. This is called a *dial-up* and is the most basic, least expensive, and slowest form of Internet connectivity. The highest speed obtainable is 56Kbps, which can be fine for emails and most text but quite slow when sending graphics or pictures or downloading large files.

The problem with analog is you can't be on the computer and be able to accept calls. You will need to jump to an ISDN line, DSL, or cable to connect to the Internet instead.

ISDN

In areas that you cannot get DSL or cable, try using ISDN, which is a little faster than analog with a speed of 128Kbps. This is a digital connection that is offered throughout most of the country. The phone company needs to install an ISDN line to your home and will usually set you up with the proper router needed or at least tell you what you need to buy.

DSL

Those of us who don't like to wait long or who work in advertising, the media, or any business where large files are sent and downloaded and time is money will want to go with high-speed Internet access such as DSL. DSL uses phone wiring to transmit information up to 143 times faster than analog. DSL is purchased at a monthly rate and requires the proper wiring and a router box from your phone company.

There are two types of DSL: ADSL and SDSL. Both are referred to as *DSL*, but their speeds are different.

Asymmetrical Digital Subscriber Line (ADSL) downloads faster (up to 8Mbps) than it uploads (up to 1Mbps), which is good for most people who are downloading files more than sending files. Symmetrical Digital Subscriber Line (SDSL) is a little faster,

> ## Caution
>
> You also need to make sure your computer is protected against hackers installing dial-up viruses that use your phone line to call long-distance and 900 numbers that can rack up unsightly charges on your phone bill. Make sure you have a good antivirus program installed on your computer system and keep it up-to-date to protect yourself against these and any other types of viruses.

downloading and uploading files at the same speed up to 1.54Mbps; it can cost a little more money than ADSL.

When DSL first came on the market, technicians came out and installed the DSL line where your computer was. Now, the phone company sends you the DSL modem to install yourself. You plug your telephone line into the DSL modem box and, for the rest of the phones in your home, you will need to connect filters to the jacks of those phones.

The downside to DSL is that your computer, when on, has an open connection to the Internet leaving it susceptible to malicious attacks. For this reason, it is important to have a firewall installed in your computer to prevent unauthorized entry to your network.

Cable

Similar to DSL, cable is another form of high-speed Internet connection that is always on. Cable high-speed Internet service is very popular in residential communities rather than businesses. Cable modems achieve a speed up to 42Mbps downloading time and 10Mbps uploading. Upon first inspection, you may think this is the fastest, but take into consideration that you are not the only person on the cable. The people in your area share it. The more people who are using their computers in your area, the more traffic on the cable line and therefore the slower the connection speed.

Since this, too, is an open connection to the Internet, you must get a firewall installed in your computer to prevent hackers from getting access to your information.

Satellite

Another form of high-speed connection is through a satellite connection that keeps the Internet always on. Many people use this type of connection when traveling across the country. Of course, you will need to travel with your satellite pointed in the right direction to receive a signal.

Wireless Internet

I have recently gone to a wireless Internet connection so I can take my laptop anywhere in my home. This is quite the luxury, especially when you do as much writing as I do.

TIP

Those who have a security alarm system installed to your homes attached to the phone system will need to have a security filter attached to the alarm system. Check with your security company for their procedures and recommendations.

TIP

Did you know that a 2.4GHZ telephone could interrupt your wireless Internet service? Me either until I kept getting bumped off of my computer. Make sure you have a corded phone or a 900MHZ or 5.8GHZ cordless phone if you have your computer hooked up to a wireless system.

To make your computer(s) wireless, you need to go to an electronics store and buy a wireless router. This router connects to your DSL modem through a thicker phone wire called an Ethernet cable.

CHECKLIST

❏ Replace rundown parts to your phone: cords, jacks, and so on.

❏ Keep a wired phone in case of power outages.

❏ Research your options for an Internet connection in your area.

❏ Contact your security system's company to make sure your DSL will not interfere with their security requirements.

❏ Use a 900MHz phone or a 5.8GHz wireless phone when using a wireless router for your computer.

Tools for the Home

The perfect date night for me would be dinner, a movie, and then a stop-off at a home center or hardware store. Call me crazy, but this gal loves her tools!

When I was an apprentice in Manhattan learning my trade as a carpenter, I was working with the finest woodworkers in the city. They taught me how to read 1/64 of an inch and how to properly use and store my tools. This is probably why I have worked hard in creating the Lyday Tool Line.

The Standard Toolset

There are tools that every homeowner should have even if you are not a do-it-yourselfer. There are problems that can occur that will need immediate attention until the pros come. I will list a set of tools that you should always have in your home. For those of you who are handier or real do-it-yourselfers, then I will add to the list.

The starter toolkit for every home should include at least the bare necessities:

- A hammer (8 oz., 13 oz., or 16 oz. is fine)
- A set of screwdrivers (some have interchangeable tips):
    - Flat tips: #1, #2, #3 (these are the various sizes)
    - Phillip's tips: #1, #2, #3
- An adjustable wrench for nuts
- Groove joint pliers (10" or 8") for plumbing pipes
- Needle-nose pliers for cutting and bending wire

Chapter 25 | Tools for the Home

- A tape measure (at least 12')
- A utility knife
- A putty knife
- A level
- A caulk gun
- Safety glasses
- A step stool (it comes in handy when you don't need a ladder)
- A 6' ladder if you don't have a step stool

For those of you who would like to add to your list of tools, include the following:

- A carpenter's handsaw or a pull saw used for cutting a piece of wood quickly without setting up a power saw. A standard carpenter's handsaw usually has a thicker blade with about 8–10 points, or teeth, per inch and works on the push stroke. A pull saw is a thinner blade with about 12 teeth to the inch and works on the pull stroke.
- Locking pliers to hold onto something that keeps getting away from you.
- A keyhole drywall saw.
- A staple gun.
- A cordless drill for light projects (6-volt or 12-volt).

> **TIP**
>
> Moisture is an enemy to your home and to your tools. Keep your tools in a dry location. You can put machine oil on a rag and lightly go over your tools to keep them in proper working condition. Always use your tools for the purpose they were meant.

DRYWALL AND WOODWORKING

If you see yourself having a good bit of drywall repairs or intend to finish a room, you will need

- Drywall knives with the following blade lengths: 3", 6", and 10"
- A utility knife with replacement blades
- A drywall saw

Those of you who will be tackling woodworking projects might consider adding the following:

- A cordless drill (12-volt or more)
- A nail set

- A prybar
- A combination square
- A miter box with a back saw
- A set of chisels
- Clamps
- Electrical tape
- A nail pouch

Power Tools

The following are power tools I suggest you have:

- A drill (12-volt or stronger).
- A jigsaw, which is the easiest saw to use and lets you see the cutting surface because of the position of the blade. It has a thin blade that won't bind when cutting curves.
- A circular saw for those more comfortable with saws. This is a strong and fast blade that rotates, cutting through heavy stock such as 2 × 4s easily.
- A reciprocating saw. It is not used often, but when you need to cut out pipes or a hole for a window, this is quite a handy saw. With different types and lengths of blades, it can saw through just about anything.
- A table saw for those who are really committed to working on projects for the home. This is a great saw for making furniture and cabinetry.
- A miter saw for woodworking enthusiasts and those who will be tackling a good bit of trim or molding. This saw gives you the option to cut an angle between 0° and 90°.

Plumbing

I always think it is a good idea to have a few plumbing tools around:

- 10" groove joint pliers and the adjustable wrench I suggested on your starter kit
- A pipe wrench, which can come in handy when stubborn joints won't budge
- A hand snake for clogged drains
- Teflon tape, a must-have

TILE PROJECTS

For those of you who would like to tackle tile projects, you should have the following:

- Carbide tile nippers
- A tile cutter
- A notched trowel for the size of tile you will be laying
- A grout float
- A large sponge
- A small scrubber sponge
- A large bucket
- Rubber gloves
- Knee pads
- A grout saw
- Measuring tape and a level from your other toolset

THE OUTDOORS

The following are tools you may need for the outdoors:

- An adjustable ladder to reach your roof
- A snow shovel, depending on the area you live in
- A leaf blower
- A lawn mower, unless you have landscapers
- A rake
- A shovel
- A set of garden tools

LAST, BUT NOT LEAST...

And don't forget the two most essential tools you will always need when doing any work around the house:

- Patience
- A sense of humor!!!

26

WALLS

I remember when I was a teenager it dawned on me one day that I had absolutely no idea what walls were made of or how they were built in the first place. I had taken for granted all of my surroundings and, for some reason on this day, this thought came crashing down around me. I'd like to tell you that I ran out and asked someone, but I didn't. Instead, when I was in my first year as an apprentice carpenter, I had a lot of silent, "oh, that's how it's done" thoughts.

WHAT ARE YOUR WALLS MADE OF?

Most walls are made of plaster, drywall, or wood paneling. An application like tiles, wallpaper, or a decorative skin coat of decorative joint compound may be applied to the top of plaster or drywall. If your walls are tile, the tile may be adhered to a cementous substructure.

Walls can last for generations, providing the house hasn't been damaged by too much moisture or water leaking in. A house that settles can cause cracks in the walls. In worst-case scenarios when the foundation starts to give away, a wall can deteriorate and become a dangerous situation.

Obviously, if your walls are crumbling, then immediately have a structural engineer assess the integrity of your foundation and home. You may need a new supporting foundation wall or other supports under a crawlspace.

For more information about your foundation, see Chapter 12, "Foundation."

If your walls have been damaged by water, you will need to repair the wall itself or, in best-case scenarios, repaint over the water marks. A wall that has been subjected to serious moisture or water might be riddled with mold.

Testing for Mold

Unfortunately, mold is becoming a major health problem for many people with allergies, asthma, or other health issues. In minor cases of mold, the area needs to be removed and any mold behind the wall must be killed. If mold has infested more than an area of about 9 square feet, you should hire a professional to remove it. The area needs to be sealed off from the rest of the home, and fans or a dehumidifier should be used to dry the area. In bathrooms and other locations where there is constant moisture, a fan should be installed to properly ventilate the room. Always address the moisture problem as well as the repair.

→ For more information about ventilating, **see** "Ventilation," **p. 119**.

Wallpaper

If you have to remove wallpaper because of water damage, you will want to buy a wallpaper serrated tool that punctures the wallpaper so a solution of water and vinegar or a wallpaper remover solution can penetrate the paper and release the adhesion. This serrated tool fits in the palm of your hand and underneath it has a couple of wheels with sharp teeth. These teeth puncture your wallpaper when you run the tool over the wallpaper, allowing a wallpaper remover solution to penetrate the paper and release the adhesion (see Figure 26.1).

Wallpaper that is not properly sized and booked before putting it on the wall can affect the longevity of the paper and also can make removal a hassle. Rent a wallpaper steamer for stubborn wallpaper removal.

If you put up wallpaper, be sure you *book* the wallpaper. When you book it, you roll on the sizing on the back of the wallpaper and then fold it, allowing the sizing to activate for a few minutes before installing it (see Figure 26.2).

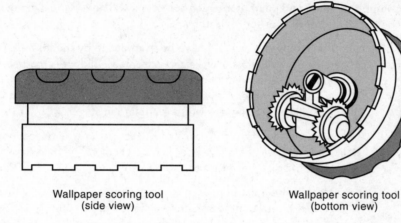

Wallpaper scoring tool
(side view)

Wallpaper scoring tool
(bottom view)

FIGURE 26.1

A serrated wallpaper tool punctures holes in the wallpaper to allow a removal solution to soak.

Cover back side with paste and fold wallpaper over on itself.

FIGURE 26.2

Booking wallpaper.

PATCHING A WALL

If you have been living in a home with a hole in the wall, now is the time to repair it. Rodents and insects can make their way through these holes, and these holes can create a draft in your home if the walls aren't insulated properly.

Repairing a patch in the wall is easy and requires the same thickness of drywall of the existing wall; in the case of plaster walls, it will need to be replastered. A quick way to tell if your walls are made of plaster or drywall is to put your hand on the wall. A cool or cold wall is a plaster wall. A wall made of drywall has a more hollow sound when knocking on it, and a plaster wall feels hard and dense against your knuckles. You can buy a patching kit that has a stick-on patch that you place over the hole and then cover with drywall compound, sand, and paint. For larger holes, you will need to use a piece of drywall for the patch and/or plaster for a plaster wall.

Plaster walls are found in older homes and have been replaced by the less expensive and less time-consuming drywall. Plaster walls are extremely solid walls made up of wood lath that is nailed horizontally on the studs with about a 1/4" space between them. Then a scratch coat layer, a brown coat layer, and finally a thin plaster layer are applied in stages.

> **NOTE**
>
> If you repair or remove a plaster wall, you will notice that some walls have hair fibers in the plaster. This is because the craftsmen who built the home or apartment building used horse or animal hair to help bind the brown coat.

Nowadays, blue board is used for plaster walls. Blue board looks just like a 4'×8' sheet of drywall but is blue in color. The blue paper allows the plaster to adhere to it to form a tight bond.

Drywall is the most popular wall material since it is so easy to work with, is fire retardant, and can be installed rather quickly. Drywall is made of gypsum and fiberglass fibers sandwiched between two layers of paper.

If you are repairing a patch or replacing an entire wall, always use drywall screws to prevent future *nail pops*, which occur when the nail backs out of the stud and the head pops through the drywall, creating a bump. Screws are less likely to pop out the way nails will. Always replace any damaged insulation with the same R-Value insulation. Use a primer and sealer over the patched area; then paint it with the same paint color and finish. For more information on painting refer to Chapter 17, "Painting."

NAIL POPS

Nail pops are a problem across the country. The term comes from the nails that hold the drywall to the studs actually popping out through the face of the drywall. The reason for this is from either a house settling or (in most cases) the wood studs drying out over time, squeezing the nail out of the wood, and pushing it out through the face of the drywall. The fix for this isn't terribly hard, but it's more of a tedious pain in the neck because there are up to 32 nails in a 4'×8' sheet of drywall. My suggestion is to pound the nail through the drywall to the stud. Then, just above it, place a drywall screw to hold the drywall to the stud and finish it off with a few coats of spackle or joint compound (see Figure 26.3). Finally, seal and paint it. You can buy nail pop kits that make this job much easier.

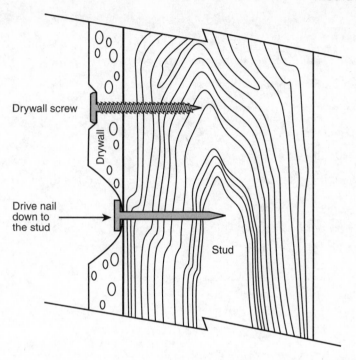

FIGURE 26.3

Fix a nail pop by pounding it flush to the stud and using a drywall screw to hold the drywall just above the nail pop.

INSULATION

Walls can only hold out so much of the chill, heat, or dampness from the outside, which is why insulation in the walls is so important. You can save yourself a bundle of money on your utility bill if you insulate your home properly. Many older homes were built without insulation and need to have insulation blown in. There are companies who specialize in this.

→ For more information about the R-Value of insulation in your area, **see** "Insulation," **p. 116**.

CHECKLIST

❑ Know what your walls are made of: plaster or drywall.

❑ Have a structural engineer diagnose major cracks or crumbling in the wall.

❑ Remove mold properly from your home.

❑ Install dehumidifiers in humid climates.

❑ Always size drywall paper before hanging it.

❑ Patch holes in your walls so rodents and insects can't crawl through them.

❑ Fix nail pops with screws.

❑ Use the proper insulation in your walls to decrease your utility bill.

Appendix A

SAFETY

I've never been one to dwell on the what-if scenarios. I guess I always feel pretty safe in my environment, but sometimes the most unthinkable can happen.

Those of you who have had a little fire in the kitchen know what I'm talking about. There have been occasions when I was cooking and the gas burner took to a paper towel or caught some grease on fire when I least expected it. Granted, a towel put it out fairly quickly, but I was glad I had a fire extinguisher near by just in case!

IN CASE OF FIRE

Every family should have a strategy to exit their home in case of a fire. I suggest everyone talk about what he or she would do and conduct practice fire drills in the home. For those living on the second level, having a fire escape ladder is smart, and family members need to have a practice run on how to get down safely on such a ladder. Again, these fire drills are important. Heaven forbid a fire occur, but if one does, you will know exactly what to do and have some assurance that the rest of your family will follow suit.

A fire needs three elements to exist: heat, oxygen, and fuel. Fuel can be gasoline, wood, or anything that burns. Heat can be disabled by putting a cup of water on a fire to bring the temperature down. However, a grease fire should not have water thrown on it since it can spread. Instead, you should use a towel or blanket to smother the fire and remove the oxygen; be careful, though, because a blanket or towel can be used as a source of fuel, too. Fuel is the hardest to remove since a house and its components are pure fuel to burn.

Fire Extinguishers

A fire extinguisher works to remove either the heat or the oxygen. Fire extinguishers are rated for the type of fires they put out. Class A extinguishers put out common combustibles such as paper, wood, and plastic. Class B extinguishers put out burning liquids such as gasoline and grease. Class C extinguishers put out electrical fires, and Class D extinguishers put out burning metal, which is rare.

A homeowner should have at least one fire extinguisher that has a multiclass rating for Class A, B, and C fires (see Figure A.1). I personally suggest having more. For instance, you should always have one hanging on the wall or someplace convenient in the kitchen. If you have a fireplace, I suggest having an extinguisher close to it. If you have multiple floors, then one on every floor is a good idea. Always have one in the workshop and garage. Fire extinguishers are very affordable and when you think how fast your life can go up in smoke, they are well worth the money spent.

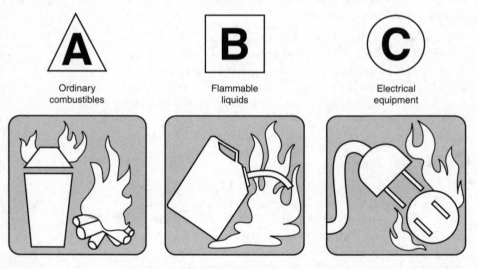

Ordinary combustibles

Flammable liquids

Electrical equipment

FIGURE A.1

The old style of labeling has the classes of fires the extinguisher puts out. The newer labels have a picture.

To use a fire extinguisher, you need to pull the pin, point the nozzle toward the fire, squeeze the operating lever, and sweep it back and forth over the fire.

Smoke Detectors

We can't put out a fire if we're not alerted that there is one; therefore, smoke detectors are very important. It's a good idea to have a few smoke detectors in your home. Always have one on each floor, including the basement. Install the smoke alarm on the ceiling or 6"–8" below it. Never keep your smoke detector on the floor because smoke rises.

Most smoke detectors last about 8–10 years. It's a good idea to put the date on the inside of the unit so you will know when you purchased it. Always buy a smoke detector that is U-L listed so you know it meets safety requirements.

Egress Windows

By code, every bedroom must have an egress window to escape a fire. An *egress window* is big enough to pass your body through it in case of a fire. The minimum measurements for the opening are a width of 20", a height of 24", and a net clearing of 5.7 square feet or 5.0 square feet at ground level. Therefore, if the width of the window were 20", then the height would need to be 42" to achieve a net clearing of 5.7 square feet. Respectively, if the height were a minimum of 24", then the width would need to be 35". The maximum sill height is 44".

> **TIP**
>
> Replace your smoke detector's batteries on the day you change your clocks (in April and October); that way, you will always know you have working batteries in your unit. This doesn't apply to smoke detectors that are hard-wired directly to an electrical system.

Carbon Monoxide

Carbon monoxide is a silent killer since you can't see it, smell it, or taste it. It can cause brain damage and, worse, kill you. There are a few ways to prevent carbon monoxide poisoning in your home. Check the color of the flame in your appliances. If the flame is orange, you've got a problem and need a professional. If you have a fireplace, check the flue to make sure there are no obstructions or birds nesting.

If you wonder whether your home has a problem, check in with yourself. Do you suffer from feeling tired and achy or have an upset stomach, dizziness, or headaches? When you go on vacation or leave for the holidays, do you feel better and invigorated? When you come back, do you start to feel bad again? You can go to your doctor to get a Cohb test. You must leave directly from your house to get this test since the carbon monoxide will deplete from your system as you get away from it.

Having a carbon monoxide detector is imperative in every home. Make sure you change your batteries every 6 months when you change your smoke detector batteries.

IN CASE OF EMERGENCY

As long as we live on this ever-changing earth, we will have to deal with natural disasters such as earthquakes, hurricanes, floods, snowstorms, and tornadoes. There's nothing we can do to prevent these events, but we can be prepared.

Safety

It's always good to have the following in case of an emergency:

- Flashlight with extra batteries

- Candles and matches

- A battery-operated radio and extra batteries

- A corded phone (not wireless)

- Water (you should have enough for each person to have 1/3 gallon of water a day for three days, so keep a gallon of water per person on hand)

- Three day's supply of food

- Can opener

- Three day's supply of pet food, if you have pets

- Toiletries and moisture wipes

- Tools, especially groove joint pliers to turn off utilities

- Cash

- First aid kit

- A generator for when the power goes out

Hurricanes

Hurricanes bring mighty winds and lots of rain. Here is a checklist for your home:

- Install truss bracing to strengthen gable end roofs.

- Check your shingles and replace any that have been damaged. Use quick-setting asphalt cement to keep your shingles in place.

- Use hurricane straps to safely keep the roof and wall connected.

- Install impact-resistant shutters. The most basic is using plywood to cover the windows or glass doors. Make sure manufactured shutters or plywood is fastened securely to the frame.

- Use a laminated window system, which is plastic that is bonded to the glass, for window or glass door protection.

- Make sure outer doors have three hinges and a deadbolt. I suggest installing head and foot bolts for inactive double-entry doors.

- Use horizontal bracing to help secure double-wide garage doors.

Tornadoes

The safest place to be in a tornado is in a community safe shelter or a tornado-safe room below ground, but many people don't have such a room. Therefore, go to the innermost room of the house away from windows. In worst-case scenarios, stay in the bathtub or under heavy furniture with a blanket around you to help protect yourself from flying debris.

Earthquakes

Earthquakes are probably the hardest to prepare for since they happen without notice. There are some things you can do to keep yourself safe:

- Use straps secured to the tops of tall furniture and then secured to a stud in the wall (you might need more than one for heavy pieces). This will help prevent tall and heavy pieces from falling over.

- Strap your water heater to the wall.

- Keep heavy objects away from your bed.

- Stay away from windows and heavy or tall furniture.

- Keep a flashlight and battery-operated radio nearby.

- Keep shoes or slippers under your bed.

- If you're inside, stay inside. If you're outside, stay there.

- Try to remain calm.

Terrorism

I regret that I have to put this section in this appendix, but I feel that it would be a great disservice after what I lived through in Manhattan on September 11th if I didn't. Basically, you should always be prepared with the items I have listed in the checklist. For information on how to survive biological, chemical, or nuclear disasters, go to the U.S. Department of Homeland Security's website (www.ready.gov).

Appendix B

SEASONAL CHECKLIST

Every season provides an opportunity for home repair or preparation for the upcoming season. This appendix is a checklist and "suggestion" appendix. If you are a first-time homeowner, you may think this is a lot to wrap your brain around. Don't worry, you'll get the swing of this within a couple of years.

FALL

- Check the house for cracks. Caulk and insulate the walls, attic, and crawlspace. Refer to Chapter 15, "Insulation and Ventilation," for more information.

- Remove screens from windows and doors.

- Install storm doors and windows.

- Check the roof for cracks around flashing and repair. Refer to Chapter 20, "Roof and Attic," for more information.

- Patch cracks in patios, driveways, and walkways. Refer to Chapter 7, "Driveways," for more information.

- Point the mortar in the brick and patch any hairline cracks in the foundation. Refer to Chapter 12, "Foundation," for more information

- Check radiators to make sure valves work properly and fix any leaks. Bleed radiators if necessary. Refer to Chapter 14, "Heating and Cooling," for more information.

- Inspect your chimney, flue, and damper. Clean them if necessary.

- Have the chimney inspected and install chimney caps. Refer to Chapter 10, "Fireplaces and Wood Stoves," for more information.

- Close the vents to basements or rooms not used.

- Check your house for entry points for rodents and plug any holes. See Appendix C, "Pest Control," for more information.

- Clean gutters and downspouts. Refer to Chapter 6, "Drainage," and Chapter 20, "Roof and Attic," for more information.

- Install gutter guards.

- Turn off outdoor sprinklers.

- Check that your snow blower is in working condition.

- Store garden hoses inside.

- Shut off the water to any outdoor spigots.

- Rake and blow leaves.

- Plant bulbs.

Winter

- Check for ice dams and water leaks.

- Insulate the attic if you didn't in the fall.

- Spray locks with silicone to prevent freezing.

- Make sure generators are in working order in case of a loss of power. Refer to Chapter 8, "Electricity," for more information.

- Buy extra candles in case of a loss of power.

- Have a user-friendly snow shovel for driveways and decks.

- Buy salt or other de-icing material.

- Feed the birds.

- Set the switch on your ceiling fan to pull air up to the ceiling.

Spring

- Remove the storm doors and windows and replace them with screens.

- Check the gutters and downspouts and remove debris.

- Check the shingles for snow or ice damage and repair them. Refer to Chapter 20 for more information.

- Replace any windows or doors that are damaged.

- Check caulking and weather stripping.

- Clean and seal driveways.

- Replace the humidifier with a dehumidifier and replace filters.

- Wash the porch, deck, and driveway. Refer to Chapter 4, "Decks and Patios," for more information.

- Wash vinyl or aluminum siding. Refer to Chapter 9, "Exterior Maintenance," for more information.

- Check the attic for rodents.

- Put winter clothes in cedar for storage.

- Check outdoor water systems.

- Change furnace and AC filters. Refer to Chapter 14 for more information.

- Replace the screens on the frames of your screen windows and doors.

- Paint the exterior of your house, if needed. Refer to Chapter 9, "Exterior Maintenance," and Chapter 17, "Painting," for more information.

- Clean your grill and check it hoses and tanks.

- Replace the lava rocks in the grill or turn ceramic briskets upside down.

SUMMER

- Water outdoor plants.

- Remove moisture with a dehumidifier.

- Check and clean ceiling fans.

- Set your switch on the ceiling fan to blow air down.

- Weed gardens.

- Prune trees. Refer to Chapter 16, "Landscape, Yard, and Garden," for more information.

- Clean dehumidifiers.

- Change the filter in HVAC units and window air conditioners.

TIP

I always forget when to change the batteries in my smoke detectors and carbon monoxide detectors. For this reason, I like to use daylight savings time (when we change our clocks in the spring and fall) as the time when I replace all of my batteries. This makes it easy to remember, and it is spaced the appropriate 6 months apart.

Appendix C

PEST CONTROL

I was an unusual child in the respect that I loved bugs, frogs, mice, and most all creatures but spiders, although I did play with many a daddy longlegs. In our attic, we had flying squirrels and I could not completely understand the need for traps. After all, they were squirrels that could fly just like in *The Adventures of Rocky and Bullwinkle*, and that feat in itself should account for a free pass even if you *are* a rodent.

It wasn't until I moved to Manhattan that I came to grips with exterminating mice. One Christmas when I lived in Chelsea, I was writing my holiday cards when I heard the sound of crunching. I turned around and noticed that a small mouse had climbed down the limb of the Christmas tree to nibble on a homemade ornament made of flour. That was cute, but it wasn't so cute when my apartment had an infestation of mice when I lived in the Lower East Side. It was then that I realized mice could make your home smell awful and bring in disease. I trapped five mice in one night with those animal-safe traps and had to walk six blocks before releasing them. What an ordeal!

Pest control is a serious matter and worth the time and money to safeguard your home.

TERMITES

Termites are probably one of the most serious pests to your home since they can jeopardize the integrity of it. This is an area I highly suggest hiring an expert to inspect your home for signs of infestation. They will give your house a thorough review and provide you a written report. Many times you would never know that your home has termites because they are very secretive insects and eat through the inside of studs and wood members.

To prevent termites, you can have a chemical soil treatment around your home to help prevent entry. Termite baiting is also effective since the termites eat the toxic bait and bring it back to the colony. The most effective way to ensure that your whole house is exterminated is to tent it, in a process known as *fumigating*. The preparation for this is fairly extensive because you need to remove all food, pets (including fish), medicine, bedding, and plants. Your house is enclosed by tarps to prevent the lethal gas from escaping, and it sits for approximately 16-30 hours.

It's important to know what types of termites your area has in order to figure out the best possible solution to exterminate or prevent them. Obviously, you should leave these methods up to the professionals, but there are three types of termites: the subterranean termite, the drywood termite, and the dampwood termite. The two that are a hazard to your home are the subterranean termite and the drywood termite.

One type of subterranean termite, the eastern subterranean termite, is found in four-fifths of the United States, reaching as far west as Utah and New Mexico and as far north as Minnesota. These termites prefer softer woods such as the pine your house is framed with. The termite nest is usually under the frost line and above the water table. The colony consists of a queen who can live up to 25 years and produce up to 2,000 eggs a DAY! Then there is a king who lives with the queen, soldiers who protect the queen, and workers who make up the larger part of the colony and whose duties include foraging for food (timber) to bring back to the colony. Termites eat the cellulose found in wood. They use tunnels to seek out food and can come into your home through expansion joints and cracks in the concrete that are 1/8" wide. They need to have humidity and moisture to live, so if you have a leaky water pipe, you have made a perfect environment for them to live in. The problem is that they are hard to detect in your home because they eat through the center of wood, therefore causing unseen structural damage.

The formosan subterranean termite is found in the southeast from Texas to South Carolina and Florida. These termites are the most aggressive and destructive since they can enter through a crack 1/6" wide and have a voracious foraging nature. These termites can eat through electrical cables, as well, causing power outages.

The western subterranean termite is found in six states from Washington to California. They are a cross between the formosan and eastern subterranean termite. They live under the ground between the frost line and water table, can crawl through cracks 1/6" wide, prefer to eat the structural timber of your home, and can eat quickly.

The desert subterranean termite is the most common subterranean termite in Arizona, but it can also be found in California and Texas. They live in desert plants and cactus and need little moisture to survive. They are quite small and can enter through a 1/32" wide crack. A sign of infestation is small drop tubes coming from the rafters or plugs of dry feces popping out of drywall. These termites build mud tubes on solid objects to travel through.

The arid-land termite can be found from the Pacific Coast east to Indiana and as far south as Mississippi. These subterranean termites are found in sand dunes and in high altitudes in the Rocky Mountains. They are the most destructive and common termites in Arizona.

The western drywood termite is slow to grow a colony. They do not live underground and prefer to live in dry wood that has less than 12% moisture. Many times humans transport them to other locations since these termites often reside in furniture.

Other Insects and Spiders

Ants, roaches, and spiders can be a real embarrassment in your home. If you have an outbreak of these critters in your home, I suggest having an exterminator come in once a month and spray your home. They will usually spray the kitchen and bathroom since those are the places where ants and roaches tend to live. For spiders, you can buy various products to help keep them at bay. It's also a good idea to spray the plants outside your home because many spiders and bugs live in your plants first before coming inside.

Always take an investigative look around your home, including the basement and crawl-space. Make sure all holes are sealed and all cracks are filled with the proper caulk. You can also buy products that plug into outlets and that swear they keep insects away.

In worst-case scenarios of bug infestation, you can bomb your home with an insecticide fogger. Make sure you protect pets (including fish), plants, and food when using these and always follow the manufacturer's directions.

Rodents

You can tell if you have mice usually by their droppings and the musty odor they create. The best way to keep rodents out of your home is to plug up any holes and cracks so they can't get in. This will take a good bit of time and lots of caulk and nonchewable matter, such as steel wool. You should make a mixture of joint compound or caulk with steel wool and put it in holes that are larger than 1/4". You will also want to keep your food in mouse-proof containers that are sealed well.

Dogs and cats may be good at killing mice and other rodents, but they are not very effective in eliminating them.

Many people have an aversion to killing rodents, yet they don't want them in their home. There are safe rodent-removing systems that will trap them; then you will need to release the mice somewhere far from your home since they are like homing pigeons and can find their way back to your house. There are products that release a smell that is unpleasant to rodents yet pleasant to humans.

For others, traps are very effective to rid your home of a few mice. You will need to place them strategically but out of harm's way from yourself and your pets. Electronic and sound devices are limited since mice will get used to the sound and become impervious to it. Poison is also effective but not a choice I would go with. I had to live in a building in the mid-1980s that used poison to kill mice living in the walls. When the mice eat the poison, they return inside the wall to die. Then your home smells of dead mouse. Yuck!

> **TIP**
>
> You can use a plastic bag as a glove. Just put your hand in the plastic bag, pick up the dead mouse, and pull the bag inside out with the mouse in it.

Always use disposable gloves when picking up a mouse or rat and tie it in a plastic bag. Then put it in another plastic bag and immediately throw it in the garbage outside.

Squirrels usually will nest in your attic. Investigate your attic and look for ways they are getting in. Most likely you will need to put in screens behind soffit vents and gable vents. This way, you will have air circulation minus the entry of squirrels or other rodents.

RACCOONS

We had raccoons in Atlanta. Matter of fact, my dad got his picture in the paper as the guy who fed the raccoons. He had names for all of them: Mamma, Jr., Socks, etc. There was a joke in the family that my mom would have to hide a cookie or banana under her blouse and take it in another room to eat it because, if my dad saw her, he'd holler, "Hey, that's the coon food." At one time there were about a dozen raccoons that would make their way from the creek up the back steps to the sliding glass doors to our house. It was there that Dad would hand-feed them. Well, the kibosh on the feeding occurred after one coon was so excited to eat a cookie that he bit down on my father's hand.

Raccoons are adorable, but they can be a nuisance and carry parasites, diseases, canine distemper, rabies, and raccoon roundworm. If you have one living in your attic, you should call the wildlife removal team in your area. Raccoons like to nest in your chimney and will leave the nest once the young are old enough to climb off the roof—generally in mid-summer. For this reason, you will want to inspect your chimney before using the fireplace.

BATS

Bats are not rodents, but mammals, and should be treated with respect. Contrary to common belief, they are not aggressive. They can live up to 20 years and give birth once a year. The downsides are that they can carry diseases and their excrement (guano) can be hazardous to your health. If you have bats in your attic, call the wildlife removal team in your area.

BIRDS

Most people don't mind birds nesting around their homes as long as they don't cause a disturbance. Chimney swifts are birds that like to nest...guess where? That's right—in your chimney. Hence, the name. Other birds and animals may take to your chimney and set up house. You want to make sure you wait until birds or any animal raises its young before removing their nests. Chimney caps should be installed and will prevent bird and animal nesting.

Appendix D

INSURANCE COVERAGE

Homeowners know that lenders make it mandatory for a homeowner to have insurance before they will lend him the money to purchase the home. Lenders are worried about the property itself, but you may want to get more than the mandated coverage. It is important to look at the worst-case scenario in dollars and cents. If your home burned to the ground, what would it cost to rebuild it and replace the contents? You will want to take into account any valuable artwork, jewelry, and rare collections you have and bump up your coverage.

THE POLICY

The insurance company considers many factors to determine the premium for the policy, such as the age of the house, its condition, its location, its square footage, the number of rooms, the number of occupants, and the materials used to build it. How you heat your home also plays a factor, along with how close you are to a fire hydrant.

There are a few ways to keep costs down. For instance, if your home is equipped with smoke detectors, alarm systems, and deadbolt locks, not only do they make your house safer, but they also help to give you a break on the cost of insurance.

Premiums will go up if you have high-risk items, such as a pool or trampoline. Nature comes with its higher premiums too—you'll pay more if you live on a coast. If you run a business out of your home, you might need to increase your liability as well because equipment, computers, and other business items can be very expensive to replace.

Homeowner's policies automatically cover furniture, appliances, clothes, and other household contents up to 40% of the amount your house is insured for. For instance, if your home has been insured for $100,000, then the contents will be insured up to $40,000.

Replacement Value Versus Actual Cash Value

Before buying homeowner's insurance, it is important to know the difference between replacement value and actual cash value. Replacement value will gives the homeowner more protection or coverage than cash value. If your home is broken into and the burglar steals your laptop, a replacement policy will cover the cost to replace your laptop. If you have a cash value policy, you will receive the money the laptop costs minus depreciation. Therefore, if your laptop is 4 years old, it will not be worth much in a cash value situation.

Always keep track of the items in your home by taking photos or using a video camera. Keep this tape or pictures in a safe place outside of your home, along with an inventory list. It's good to keep them in two separate places: a bank and a friend's home. It's a good idea to copy receipts of expensive items as well.

Coverage for Disaster

If you live in an area where there are hurricanes, tornadoes, earthquakes, or flooding, you should consider extra insurance for such disasters. Flood insurance is not covered in a regular homeowner's policy. You will need to seek specific flood insurance from National Flood Insurance Program (NFIP) or from a local insurance company that offers flood insurance. Earthquakes require separate insurance, too.

Other information you should find out is whether you have insurance to cover medical expenses if someone accidentally injures herself inside your home and what protection you have against liability claims. Look into additional living expenses coverage if your home becomes uninhabitable after a covered loss.

And lastly, make sure all of your structures are covered in your home policy. A friend of mine had to learn the hard way when he lost a barn and three other structures on his land from fire. Unfortunately, he did not have enough coverage to rebuild the buildings. This goes for your landscape as well—if you have expensive trees and shrubs, then you may need to get landscape insurance.

It is wise to assess your home with the thought of a worst-case scenario. You can then take into consideration the reality of what you will need to replace concerning your home and possessions. I suggest you write down questions to ask your insurance company so that you are very clear as to what is covered and how much money you are covered for.

Index